Boston Playwrights' Theatre
at Boston University Presents

Boston Theatre Marathon of Ten-Minute Plays Volume V

Baker's Plays
7611 Sunset Blvd.
Los Angeles, CA 90042
BAKERSPLAYS.COM

NOTICE

This book is offered for sale at the price quoted only on the understanding that, if any additional copies of the whole or any part are necessary for its production, such additional copies will be purchased. The attention of all purchasers is directed to the following: this work is fully protected under the copyright laws of the United States of America, the British Commonwealth, including Canada, and all other countries of the Copyright Union. Violations of the Copyright Law are punishable by fine or imprisonment, or both. The copying or duplication of this work or any part of this work, by hand or by any process, is an infringement of the copyright and will be vigorously prosecuted.

This play may not be produced by amateurs or professionals for public or private performance without first submitting application for performing rights. Royalties are due on all performances whether for charity or gain, or whether admission is charged or not. Since performance of this play without the payment of the royalty fee renders anybody participating liable to severe penalties imposed by the law, anybody acting in this play should be sure, before doing so, that the royalty fee has been paid. Professional rights, reading rights, radio broadcasting, television and all mechanical rights, etc. are strictly reserved. Application for performing rights should be made directly to BAKER'S PLAYS.

No one shall commit or authorize any act or omission by which the copyright of, or the right to copyright, this play may be impaired. No one shall make any changes in this play for the purpose of production.

Publication of this play does not imply availability for performance. Both amateurs and professionals considering a production are strongly advised in their own interest to apply to Baker's Plays for written permission before starting rehearsals, advertising, or booking a theatre.

Whenever the play is produced, the author's name must be carried in all publicity, advertising and programs. Also, the following notice must appear on all printed programs, "Produced by special arrangement with Baker's Plays."

Licensing fees for *BOSTON THEATRE MARATHON OF TEN-MINUTE PLAYS, VOLUME V* is based on a per performance rate and payable one week in advance of the production.

Please consult the Baker's Plays website at www.bakersplays.com or our current print catalogue for up to date licensing fee information.

Copyright © 2010 by Baker's Plays
Made in U.S.A. All rights reserved.

BOSTON THEATRE
MARATHON OF TEN-MINUTE PLAYS, VOLUME V
ISBN 978-0-87440-317-6

#1586-B

MUSIC USE NOTE

FOREWORD

On Sunday, April 13, 2003, the Boston Theater Marathon continued its sold-out annual run at the Boston Playwrights' Theatre—on BPT's two black box stages. Dozens of actors and directors moved from one theatre to the other (switching places from one hour to the next), performing 45 imaginative, distinctly different, hilarious, sad, inventive and wonderful ten-minute plays for our packed houses. And each one was supported by a different New England theater company. It doesn't get better than this! It was fly-by-the-seat-of-your-pants theatre: the technical crew moved through the SRO crowds with couches, chairs, lamps, and boxes to arrange each new world every ten-minutes; the actors, waiting to enter on cue, stood in line next to audience members waiting for seats. The energy was indescribable—just like these challenging and worthy plays. You had to be there.

Once again, these works were culled from well over 300 submissions from playwrights all over New England. Wonderful gifts from theatre companies and theatre artists were raffled off during the day, culminating at 10 P.M. with a blast-out party containing the best schmoozing found in six states. Because of the ever-generous donation from The Humanities Foundation at Boston University, once again we were able to give all of our proceeds to the Theatre Community Benevolent Fund—a non-profit charity organization established to give emergency funds to theatre folk in need.

These plays are as different as the writers and the companies who produced them. They range from out-of-the-world farce to the tragic, from somber to silly, from meaningful to...well, they're always meaningful. I hope you will enjoy reading these tasty "snacks" as much as I did watching them.

With warmest regards,

Kate Snodgrass
Artistic Director
Boston Theater Marathon V

TABLE OF CONTENTS

THE ORNITHOLOGIST'S MOTHER

By Jake Strautman

CHARACTERS

Tedesco

Ewing

Sutton

(**TEDESCO** *stands centerstage looking stage right through a theodolite on a tripod. He has a clipboard and writes down his calculations. He refers to a second clip board several times. A bird chirps off right. He pulls out a pair of binoculars and scans the area off-right, nothing.* **EWING** *sneaks quietly on stage left. He puts down a pail he is carrying and carefully aims a shotgun at* **TEDESCO**. **TEDESCO** *squints again through the theodolite, takes out a pair of binoculars and observes the bird.*)

TEDESCO. Hello, momma bird.

(**EWING** *makes a birdcall.* **TEDESCO** *pans across the audience looking for the bird.* **EWING** *calls again. He is crouched down.* **TEDESCO** *pans until he is facing* **EWING** *but obviously looking in the trees for the bird.* **EWING** *calls again.* **TEDESCO** *slowly brings the binoculars down, brings them into focus, and drops his clipboard.*)

TEDESCO. Don't shoot! I'm the surveyor.

EWING. You from the city?

TEDESCO. That's quite a convincing birdcall you have. I thought you were from the family Ictusiad, genus Oriolus, rare in these parts.

EWING. You from the courthouse?

TEDESCO. Yes – no – yes, I spend most of my days outdoors. Is this your land?

EWING. Yes, by God.

TEDESCO. A wonderful assortment of undergrowth, plenty of nest-making possibilities.

EWING. It's too dry.

TEDESCO. Droughts are very dry, but to the female burrowing brown-wing, paradise.

(**EWING** *begins to lower the gun.*)

Are you Mr. Ewing's son?

9

EWING. Don't know *Mr.* Ewing. It's just Momma and me.

TEDESCO. You're Mrs. Ewing's son.

EWING. *Miss* Ewing, yes. I'm Darren.

TEDESCO. Darren, I'm here to settle the dispute between the Ewing and the Sutton land. My name is –

EWING. *(raising the rifle)* Sutton land! You calling this Sutton land?

TEDESCO. No – yes – no. I'm here to make a fair and impartial assessment based on these most accurate measurements and the previous deeds' descriptions. Since Mr. Sutton is taking you and your momma to court over a border dispute, he's invited me on his, I mean *the* disputed land. When neither of you answered your doors, I left a notice in both your mailboxes.

EWING. *(lowering the rifle)* That's why I came down –

TEDESCO. I appreciate the company –

EWING. To see that you're making a "fair assessment," understand?

TEDESCO. Oh, you don't have to worry; I'm an elected official. You may have seen my name on the ballot…I'm Jeremy Tedesco –

EWING. Where were you born?

TEDESCO. In Pennsylvania, but my mother moved us to Marshall County when I was very small –

EWING. Just your mother?

TEDESCO. Yes.

EWING. Pleasure to meet you, Mr. Tedesco.

TEDESCO. You're welcome to watch, but I have to do these boring triangulations, work, work, work. I wish I could keep my same job but without all this measuring. You know? Daylight's a-wasting, and the topo map is off something awful.

(EWING sits and watches him.)

Beautiful country you've got here.

EWING. Land's nothing without water.

TEDESCO. *(looking through binoculars)* That is a beautiful waterfall, the rocks, each a bubbling bath, a tiny little ecosphere.

EWING. Are you looking at that goddamn fence Sutton strung across the run?

TEDESCO. No, I'm confirming the angle measurements.

EWING. Well.

TEDESCO. I'm looking. The new one right before the stream...with the section cut out.

EWING. Did that with a pair of shears. Sutton can't build a fence anyhow.

TEDESCO. It's rather straight, it looks like.

EWING. Yeah, straight across my momma's land. How is she supposed to do the wooshing, or take a bath if she wants to?

TEDESCO. Your well?

EWING. Dried up last week. Right here's the only water source this side of the ridge and it belonged to my Momma's side of the family long before Sutton bought up all that land he don't use.

TEDESCO. So it does belong to Sutton?

EWING. Watch it, surveyor. You'll make a fair assessment and soon, then git off my land, then I'll take my momma this bucket full of Ewing-water for her cookin'.

TEDESCO. I understand, Darren.

(He looks back into the theodolite. A different bird calls from stage-right. TEDESCO picks up binoculars and looks.)

Shhh! That's not a grey-breasted tweaking titty-mouse...Where is he? There there.

(SUTTON comes out from behind a tree with his gun aimed at EWING who raises his gun in return. They inch closer. TEDESCO continues talking, obliviously.)

EWING. Mr. Surveyor –

TEDESCO. *(whispering)* Shhh! Birds are amazing creatures. They have different songs for different times of day, ways of telling each other of danger.

(**EWING** and **SUTTON** *begin a slow circling.*)

EWING. Mr. Surveyor, sir –

TEDESCO. Whether it's coming in fast or stalking them nice and slow. Oh. Not even an adolescent male, never heard of one so far north, must be the climate change, and a young one at that – oh, my goodness, still has his face fuzz, all by his lonesome. Darren, do your bird call again. I bet you wouldn't believe it if I told you. I never really wanted to be a surveyor. My whole life I just wanted to draw birds. My mother made me study maths in school. He's beautiful. Tweak Tweak! Darren, Darren!

SUTTON. On a first name basis already. You Ewings don't know when to stop weasling away at my land. I call in the county and here you are all jovial-like. Makes me sick.

EWING. I ain't been here five minutes. You're the "truss-passer." Who strings a 100 feet of barb wire stretching across my path to the new swimming hole? There's your proof of wrong-doing. Mr. Tedesco is come to vindicate me and my Momma.

(**SUTTON** *aims his gun at* **TEDESCO.**)

TEDESCO. Mr. Sutton, I presume.

SUTTON. Just call me Sutton.

TEDESCO. Sutton. If you'll lower your weapons, both of you, for a moment, I can start to figure this border problem out, and I'm not taking either side. I'm just here to do the surveying, but I can't concentrate on triangulation looking down the barrels of two hunting rifles.

SUTTON. Ha! Hunting rifle, why this is just my bird pellet gun.

EWING. Yeah. My hunting rifle's double-barreled. This is my crow picker.

TEDESCO. Bird pellets? Crow picker?

SUTTON. Didn't know the size of the jailbird down here, guess I should have brought the heavy artillery.

TEDESCO. You two kill birds?

SUTTON. I'll take out anything that gits near my roses. They's not easy to grow during a drought.

EWING. Same goes for me and Momma's corn.

SUTTON. Is that why you're down here muddying up my pristine mountain spring? To water a useless row of corn?

EWING. You don't have no use for your water, you don't even have a real garden.

SUTTON. Spying on top of trespassing is it? You're my witness, and it's an award-winning rose garden. Twice it was in the Tab.

EWING. Roses! You can't eat them. Who made you plant those, your Momma?

SUTTON. *(wielding his gun)* Never speak ill of my Momma, God rest her.

EWING. I'm sorry to hear she's passed on.

(They circle again. The new bird repeats its call.)

TEDESCO. Shhhh. Hello, little orphan boy. I didn't forget about you. Tweak. Tweak. Don't mind the scary men.

SUTTON. What's he doing? You better get back to work. My tax dollars are paying for this.

TEDESCO. I'm not doing any work until you both drop the rifles, er bird guns. Can I have a moment for a quiet sketch? This is very exciting.

(He pulls out a sketch pad.)

SUTTON. What's he drawin'?

EWING. Some bird. You heard him. His Momma wouldn't let him be a bird painter or drawer.

SUTTON. Oh. Bird painter? What's that called in Latin?

EWING. What are you talking about?

SUTTON. There's a fancy city term for it. Bird-o-grapher or something.

EWING. Bird-o-grapher! How about Wren-brandt!

(EWING laughs heartily. SUTTON is dismayed.)

SUTTON. Laugh you scrawny pigeon, but I bet my eyes are twice as good as you – and you half my age.

EWING. You want to prove it.

SUTTON. Yeah.

(*They look around for something to shoot.*)

SUTTON. Well, what are we shootin' at boy. Wait. I got it. See that little bird up there the fellow's drawing? I'll give you first shot. If after you miss, and I don't clip him neither, then I'll still call you the better man. Hell, I'll give you part of this run you're stealing from, but only 'cause of your momma.

EWING. You can't give what ain't yours.

SUTTON. Go ahead, I'm right behind you.

(*They both aim at the bird.*)

TEDESCO. Thank you, little orphan bird. Now back to work.... What the hell's going on? Mr. Sutton! Mr. Ewing! You can both stand guard if you wish, but if anyone, anyone shoots the grey-breasted titty-mouse, I might just find that my angles are off to the benefit of the non-bird killing party! Understand?

(*They lower their guns and stand on either side.*)

TEDESCO. Fifteen-point-five degrees Northeast toward the silver maple. I did that. Now, I've shot the Sutton line.

SUTTON. Shot what?

TEDESCO. That's what we call it, shooting the line. Do you mind? Eighty-four-point-five degrees from the Oak. And now I've got the Ewing line set. But for the two lines to match up...and here's what's stranger, the topo map is all haywire.

EWING. Topo?

TEDESCO. Topographical.

SUTTON. I knew that.

EWING. Is that like show you the hills and valleys?

TEDESCO. The elevation, yes.

SUTTON. Would you let the man work? He's about to prove you and your momma as liars.

EWING. You calling my momma a liar?

SUTTON. You Ewings are all the same, going way back to Eugene Ewing, making up stuff to gain new land.

EWING. Say it again! The new swimming hole is mine. I need it. I use it. You sprinkle it on your flower garden, what use is that? I don't care if your mother did plant it.

SUTTON. How dare you say that: that garden was the thing Momma was proudest of. In the final days, she would look up at me and say, "I look like the last rose o'summer." That's what she used to say. She was always thinking of her garden in the end. I go to give my roses their daily drink of mountain spring water, cool and fresh running down the hill from right chere spot, and it's filled with silt and muddier than the Ohio. So, I come to see what's going on. And there you are filling your bucket in the new swimming hole on my land!

TEDESCO. Did you say "new" swimming hole?

(He looks again at his chart.)

EWING. That's Ewing land you're claiming.

SUTTON. You want to throw down pigeon boy?

EWING. I'll throw down.

(They toss their guns and start to wrestle.)

TEDESCO. Fellows. Guys. Hey! Both of your deeds are completely wrong.

SUTTON. The county sure ain't taking my land.

EWING. You said it, Sutton. The state took my momma's coal from under her. We had to dig a second well.

SUTTON. Swindled! Swindled we were. Our well went dry as bark. Company bastards try to repay us with...

TEDESCO. Wait, wait! There's a coalmine under here?

EWING. Yep.

SUTTON. It's the county's fault.

(SUTTON and EWING stop wrestling and advance on TEDESCO.)

TEDESCO. Fellows, now, I think I figured it out.

(*A baby bird squawks with intensity.*)

TEDESCO. Uh – fellows – (*more squawks*)

(**TEDESCO** *turns and looks through the binoculars.* **EWING** *and* **SUTTON** *look at each other.*)

Oh no, he's trying to fly. He's got no mother to help him. He's going to....

(*All three follow the bird's fall from the nest.*)

EWING. Is it okay?

SUTTON. I think I'm going to be sick.

TEDESCO. Quick, Sutton, give me your jacket. Ewing, I need something to hold the poor thing in.

(**EWING** *hands him his pail.* **TEDESCO** *runs off stage.* **SUTTON** *and* **EWING** *watch with frustration.*)

EWING. (*calling to* **TEDESCO**) He's there. Beneath that silver maple.

SUTTON. No, it's the next one over. You got him.

TEDESCO. (*offstage*) He's still alive!

EWING. He'd be in much better shape if you hadn't shot his momma.

SUTTON. I never shot his momma. I don't think. Didn't you say you picked off a few birds yourself?

(**TEDESCO** *enters with the bucket.*)

EWING. Maybe I did.

TEDESCO. It's okay baby bird. I'm not going to hurt you.

(**TEDESCO** *continues to coo to the bird, but* **EWING** *and* **SUTTON** *take the pail and begin nurturing.*)

EWING. We can walk him up to my place. My Momma will know what to do.

SUTTON. He fell on my land. At least you can accept that. Besides, I might owe it to his...family...Ya'll come down to my place. I got some milk and bread we can feed it.

EWING. Yeah. We might owe it that.

TEDESCO. Careful. Careful.

(SUTTON *and* EWING *begin offstage with the bird.*)

SUTTON. You coming County-man?

TEDESCO. Yes – no – yes, fellows, I haven't finished here yet. The coal mines must have shifted the elevation and the water table, but the property markers are gone and the topo map is...

EWING. Sutton, I've got to come down here for water on Mondays and Thursdays, for Momma, if you understand.

SUTTON. It's for your momma. Of course I understand. I'll water my momma's roses on Saturdays, Wednesdays, and ... uh...when the mountain stream is the clearest, now that I know your bathing schedule.

TEDESCO. Can you guys help me gather my equipment?

EWING/SUTTON. No problem. Here take my gun.

(TEDESCO *is loaded down with guns.* EWING *and* SUTTON *begin to exit carrying bucket, theodolite and flags.*)

SUTTON. So, tell me Mr., how did you get into this surveying business.

TEDESCO. My daddy left us across the Pennsylvania state line.

SUTTON. I'm sorry to hear that.

EWING. But why did your daddy leave?

TEDESCO. Oh, he was fond of the boops.

SUTTON. I'm sorry...what is a...?

TEDESCO. A fish. Mediterranean. But, like I was saying, my mother was a beautiful woman...

EWING/SUTTON. Uh-huh. Amen. Mine too. Eyes of Mary, etc..

(*All exit. Lights out.*)

ECKSTEIN & SONS

By Alan Brody

CHARACTERS

CARL ECKSTEIN – Late thirties.
MAURY ECKSTEIN – His grandfather, late seventies.

(*SETTING*: *The Showroom of Eckstein Quality Clothiers, around 1:30 p.m.*)

(*AT RISE*: *On stage there is rack of suits, a shelf of shirts and a counter.* **CARL ECKSTEIN** *is on his cell phone.*)

CARL. How much? I couldn't have heard you right...How could I have lost that much? Two weeks ago I had... Jesus, Hal. You're breaking my balls here...Yeah, yeah, yeah. Buy now when shares are cheap. I heard that before...Where am I going to get the money?...I tell you what...I tell you what, Hal. You show me a port-folio going up for a change and I'll throw my money into it...Don't jerk me off. It's hemorrhaging...You know something, Hal?...You know something?...I don't give a shit that it's happening to everybody else. It's happening to me. I tell you what...I tell you what, Hal...You show me some improvement in two weeks or I liquidate and turn it all into suits and shirts...I'm saying good-bye now...A customer just came in. I'm saying good-bye...Good-bye, Hal.

(**CARL** *punches off and calls offstage.*)

CARL. Grandpa! I need you!

MAURY. (*offstage*) I got a sleeve.

CARL. Take the pins out of your mouth.

MAURY. (*off*) When I'm finished.

CARL. I've got to get out of here.

MAURY. (*off*) Where's the girl?

CARL. Lunch.

MAURY. (*off*) All right. I'm finished.

(**MAURY ECKSTEIN** *enters from the back room. He has a tape measure around his neck and holds a suit jacket with pinned sleeves.*)

MAURY. These new fabrics. Look at this. It makes me ashamed to do alterations.

CARL. That's top of the line.

MAURY. The line is very low.

CARL. Sidney Rickoff loves that suit. He told me he's going to wear it to the World Trade Organization conference.

MAURY. What's he doing there?

CARL. As far as I'm concerned, he's wearing our clothes.

MAURY. You want me to embroider Eckstein Quality Clothiers on the back like a T-shirt?

CARL. I'll be back in an hour.

MAURY. Can I say something as a grandfather instead of as an employee who gave you the business in the first place?

CARL. You gave it to my father. He gave it to me.

MAURY. As a grandfather I have something to say.

CARL. All right.

MAURY. What I have to say is, where are you going?

CARL. Grandpa…

MAURY. A woman or a bar?

CARL. You wouldn't understand.

MAURY. I built this business from a pack on my back. You think I still live in the Garden of Eden?

CARL. I'm going to the bank.

MAURY. A girl or a bar would be better.

CARL. You didn't talk like that five years ago when I was buying all the new locations.

MAURY. As a matter of fact, I did. You weren't listening.

CARL. I've made my money work for all of us.

MAURY. Why should money work for us? I always thought we were supposed to work for money.

(**CARL** *goes to the rack.*)

CARL. What's this?

MAURY. What?

CARL. This suit.

MAURY. A return.

CARL. This fabric looks ten years old.

MAURY. Twenty-five. Seymour Schiff. He came in this morning. He was upset the fabric wore out.

CARL. Twenty-five years.

MAURY. I always guaranteed my fabrics.

CARL. You gave him his money back?

MAURY. I exchanged.

CARL. What did you give him?

MAURY. The suit that was there.

CARL. That was mohair!

MAURY. It's a hard fabric to work on.

CARL. You altered it.

MAURY. Seymour's got a difficult build. Always did.

CARL. This has got to stop.

MAURY. What does?

CARL. This crazy business of...

MAURY. Honor. It's called honor, Carl. I gave the man my guarantee.

CARL. This is just why I keep you in the back. I can't trust you out here.

MAURY. You can trust the girl? She doesn't know synthetic from natural.

CARL. She's not going to wipe me out with integrity.

MAURY. What are you doing at the bank?

CARL. I'm taking out a loan.

MAURY. Another one.

CARL. I'm in control.

MAURY. This isn't the time for another location.

CARL. It's not for that.

MAURY. What, then? Not more stock.

CARL. Hal says it's a good time to buy.

MAURY. I'll tell you something, I think you've got a gambling problem.

CARL. Investment isn't gambling.

(**MAURY** *shrugs.*)

CARL. Don't shrug like that. You know it makes me crazy when you shrug like that.

MAURY. How much money did you lose last year?

CARL. None.

MAURY. None.

CARL. It's all on paper. I just have to hold on, I'll make an incredible profit.

MAURY. That'll be on paper, too. What does Rita think of all this?

CARL. She trusts me.

MAURY. She doesn't know.

CARL. Should I consult the kids, too?

MAURY. It wouldn't hurt. What's your collateral? You've already used the Perth Amboy.

(*No answer.*)

MAURY. This place?

CARL. It's not a big deal.

MAURY. This place?

CARL. I'm not going to default.

MAURY. You've paid off the Perth Amboy?

CARL. You never cared about the Perth Amboy, anyway.

MAURY. I care about this place.

CARL. I'm taking out a loan. I'm not trashing the store.

MAURY. Why don't you use Rita as collateral? Or the boys? Put them at risk.

CARL. Don't be unreasonable.

MAURY. This place is my child. As much as your father was, may he rest in peace. And you know there's a risk.

CARL. You have to take risks to win.

MAURY. What's winning?

CARL. Everything I do is good for the business.

MAURY. A spotless reputation is good for the business.

CARL. *(with too much sincerity)* I know. You've taught me that. It was an important lesson.

MAURY. Don't patronize me.

CARL. All right. It's the twentieth century. Get used to it.

MAURY. Something happened to decency when the number at the end of the century changed?

CARL. Everything I'm doing is decent.

MAURY. It's legal. Decent includes human feelings.

CARL. I have feelings. I care about Rita, the kids…

MAURY. And me?

CARL. Of course, you.

MAURY. I wondered. Because more and more lately, I've been feeling like an employee who might be downsized.

CARL. I've got twenty-five people in each of the other locations. There's just you, me, and the girl here. How could I downsize you?

MAURY. This place is why you have twenty-five people at the other ones. This is Eckstein's Quality Clothiers. The other places are trafe. Fast food shirts and suits. Even the people who never heard of me or your father, may he rest in peace, go to those other places because of this store. This is where honor and quality started.

CARL. What do you want from me?

MAURY. Stay here. I'll buy us lunch. We can sit here and talk over bagels and cream cheese. Maybe a white fish.

CARL. I don't have time.

MAURY. No, my precious grandson. I'm the one who doesn't have time. Sit down. We'll talk first and eat later. If we feel like it.

CARL. I can't…

MAURY. *(sharply now)* Sit down! (CARL *hesitates*) I'll report you to the union.

CARL. What union?

MAURY. Me. I just made myself a chapter. Sit! *(CARL sits)* From the time you were pishing in your diapers, I couldn't make up my mind. I picked you up and held you in my arms and my blood turned to love flowing through my body. That didn't stop me from seeing the way you held your little fists tight like this.

(MAURY looks down at CARL's fists that are balled up as described. CARL realizes, opens them, but too late.)

MAURY. And that's how it's been for thirty-eight years. I let your father, may he rest in peace, deal with it when he was alive. It left me free to love you. He could slap you down when you said rude things to your grandmother, may she rest in peace, and me. He could go down to the police station when your school complained you were selling marijuana in the halls— and he could be the one who could believe you when you said it was oregano.

CARL. It was.

MAURY. It wasn't. And if it was? There you were, already selling shoddy goods. No, when he died, I had to give up my grandparent's privilege of unconditional love. And by then it was too late. No way to reach you. Loyalty? Old-fashioned. Ethics? Sentimental. Personal honor? A frill. And frankly I shudder for my great grandchildren.

CARL. I keep them in the best clothes. I feed them the best food.

MAURY. And you'll do anything to keep it that way. They're growing up thinking the most important thing in the world is the best clothes and the best food. Soon they're going to be connoisseurs of the best drugs.

CARL. Kevin is ten years old, for Chrissake.

MAURY. I knew you were going to be a heartless, self-interested little putz when you were eight.

CARL. Why are you doing this?

MAURY. I got no power, Carl. I gave my life to your father and he gave it to you. I'm telling you that whether or not you downsize me, you've shut me out of my own life. You should know that.

CARL. Dad and I made sure you had a good pension.

MAURY. And that took care of everything.

CARL. I don't know what you want from me!

MAURY. Wait for me to die before you go to the bank again.

CARL. You're manipulating me.

MAURY. No, Carl. I'm begging.

CARL. It's a question of timing, Grandpa.

MAURY. And that's all you can say.

CARL. I never know how to talk to you.

(*MAURY nods in agreement.*)

CARL. I'm going.

(*CARL starts out. Stops.*)

CARL. Aren't you going to stop me?

MAURY. With what?

(*CARL leaves. MAURY goes to the old suit and examines it expertly.*)

MAURY. Maybe I could still get something out of this.

(*HE starts to snip the seams…*)

END

AIRPORT HELL

by Robert Brustein

CHARACTERS

Eurydice
Airport Attendant

The Boston Theatre Marathon production of *AIRPORT HELL* was directed by David Wheeler and included:

EURYDICE . . . . Paula Plum
AIRPORT ATTENDANT . . . . Karen Macdonald

(A check-in desk in an airport terminal. A desk sign with the motto "Delta is Ready When You Are." A pleasant female ATTENDANT is busy on the phone. EURYDICE WATSON, carrying a large bag and a carry-on, comes up to sign in.)

EURYDICE. Miss?

ATTENDANT. I'll be with you in a moment. *(to the phone)* Well, why wouldn't she leave him? This is the fifth time he's cheated on her in a month. *(to EURYDICE)* This won't take a moment.

EURYDICE. *(pleasant)* My plane is leaving in forty minutes. I have to check in. And there are long lines at security.

ATTENDANT. What plane is that?

EURYDICE. Flight 5802 to Tampa.

ATTENDANT. Oh, that flight's been cancelled. They didn't phone you?

EURYDICE. Cancelled? Why?

ATTENDANT. They never tell us. Could be weather. Could be equipment.

EURYDICE. But I have to get to Tampa today. My daughter is having a baby.

ATTENDANT. Really? Boy or girl?

EURYDICE. They think it's a baby girl.

ATTENDANT. Isn't that precious? What are they going to name her?

EURYDICE. I'm sorry. I'm in a hurry.

ATTENDANT. Of course you are. Listen, I can't help you, but I suggest you take the airport shuttle over to United at Terminal C. They have dozens of flights to Tampa.

EURYDICE. Thank you. You've been very kind.

ATTENDANT. *(The ATTENDANT goes back to her phone call).* So tell her to chuck the bum out of the house, and find herself another guy.

(**EURYDICE** *wanders in circles with her luggage as the* **ATTENDANT** *changes her desk card to "Fly the Friendly Skies of United."*)

EURYDICE. I have a flight to Tampa today and the woman at Delta said…

ATTENDANT. *(not friendly)* Wait a minute. Please go to the back of the line.

EURYDICE. What line? I'm the only passenger here.

ATTENDANT. You jumped the queue. There are hundreds of other passengers waiting to check in, unless you are a First Class passenger, a Silver Wings Plus, or can fake a disability.

EURYDICE. I do have a disability. *(She pretends to limp.)* I sprained my ankle.

ATTENDANT. All right. I'll take you then. You're going to Tampa you say? How many bags to check?

EURYDICE. Just this one.

(The **ATTENDANT** *takes it and puts it on the roller.)*

ATTENDANT. Yes, United does have a flight to Tampa, leaving at 2:15 PM. Give me your Delta ticket. *(She rips it up.)*

EURYDICE. That's great.

ATTENDANT. But it only flies on alternate Tuesdays, Thursdays, and Saturdays, except for Thanksgiving weekend, Gay Pride Week, and Shevouth, when it flies on alternate Mondays, Wednesdays, and Fridays. Unfortunately, today is Sunday, when there is no flight to Tampa. I suggest you try American in Terminal B. I believe they have a flight to Tampa this afternoon.

EURYDICE. But you've ripped up my ticket.

ATTENDANT. Not to worry. The ticket is in the computer.

EURYDICE. And you've checked my luggage.

ATTENDANT. Yes, to Tampa. Aren't you going there?

EURYDICE. On another plane.

ATTENDANT. Well, the bag would have been lost anyway. (*proudly*) We misplace 10,000 pieces of baggage every day. Isn't that impressive? Here, fill out a claim check.

EURYDICE. Never mind. It's just a lot of baby things, and presents. I kept all my personal items in my carry-on.

ATTENDANT. Very smart. I never check bags myself.

(**EURYDICE** *rolls her carry-on around in ever-widening circles, as the* **ATTENDANT** *changes the desk card to "American Airlines: Getting There is Half the Fun."*)

EURYDICE. I was told that you might have a ticket for me on a flight to Tampa. I was on Delta Flight 5456 but the plane got cancelled.

ATTENDANT. We are flying to Tampa today, at 2:45 PM, Flight 376.

EURYDICE. Thank God.

ATTENDANT. But the plane is presently full.

EURYDICE. Oh, no.

ATTENDANT. I'd be happy to put you on a waiting list. We often get cancellations.

EURYDICE. Oh, all right.

ATTENDANT. Your best bet is to call the airline directly. They sometimes put seats aside. Here's the number. Do you have a cell phone?

EURYDICE. Yes.

(*She dials it. The same* **ATTENDANT** *answers the phone.*)

PHONE VOICE. Welcome to American Airlines, where getting there is half the fun. For English, press one. Para hablar en Espanol, numero dos. (**EURYDICE** *presses "one."*) For bankruptcy claims, press one. For oversold flights, press two. For sexual harrassment by the steward, press three. For trashed, drenched, and mutilated luggage, press four. For all other miseries, press five. (**EURYDICE** *quickly presses "five."*) We're sorry. All of our representatives are currently busy with other customers. Please stay on the line. Your call is very important to us. (*Bad music plays.* EURYDICE *shakes the phone in frustration*).

EURYDICE. If it's so damned important, then answer the goddamned phone.

PHONE VOICE. Did you swear at me?

EURYDICE. No, just talking to myself.

PHONE VOICE. Then how can I help you?

EURYDICE. I'm told you have a plane leaving for Tampa in a few hours, Flight 376. But it's full.

PHONE VOICE. Let me see. Yes, we do have a single seat on Flight 376. Do you want it?

EURYDICE. Please!!!

PHONE VOICE. Name?

EURYDICE. Eurydice Watson.

PHONE VOICE. Credit card number?

EURYDICE. Yes, it's American Express 55603-80589-3012890

PHONE VOICE. Expires?

EURYDICE. 05/21/06.

PHONE VOICE. You expire today.

EURYDICE. Today?!!!

PHONE VOICE. Let me read this back to you.

EURYDICE. Please don't bother. Just ticket me. I'm going to be late.

PHONE VOICE. All right, you have one seat on Flight 346 to Tampa, Florida, leaving at 2:45 PM this afternoon and arriving at 1:45 PM.

EURYDICE. Wait a minute. How can the plane arrive before it leaves?

PHONE VOICE. That's just what it says here.

EURYDICE. That it leaves at 2:45 PM and arrives at 1:45 PM?

PHONE VOICE. Maybe there's a time change?

EURYDICE. (*beginning to lose it*) The plane is going to Florida for Christ sake and leaving from Boston. How can there be a time change?

PHONE VOICE. Oh, I see the problem. That plane has been diverted to Kuala Lumpur, Malaysia. It arrives at 1:45 PM the next day. I knew there was a time change.

EURYDICE. What about Tampa.

PHONE VOICE. All our Tampa flights have been temporarily rerouted today to Kuala Lumpur, Malaysia.

EURYDICE. What do I have to do to get to Florida today? Please help me? My daughter is having a baby!

PHONE VOICE. Go to the reservation desk. *(And she hangs up.)*

*(**EURYDICE** wanders back to the American Airlines **ATTENDANT**.)*

ATTENDANT. Any luck?

EURYDICE. No, all the flights to Tampa have been temporarily rerouted to Kuala Lumpur, Malaysia.

ATTENDANT. Listen, I've been looking at the schedules, and your best bet is this new low fare airline at Terminal X called Limbo Airlines. They have regular flights to all the southern cities.

EURYDICE. I didn't know there was a Terminal X.

ATTENDANT. At the very extreme end of the airport.

EURYDICE. *(at the end of her rope)* You've been very kind.

ATTENDANT. No problem.

*(**EURYDICE** wheels her carry-on round and round in circles until the **ATTENDANT** changes the name tag to "Limbo Airlines: It's Worth the Wait.")*

ATTENDANT. Hello, we've been waiting for you. Welcome to Limbo Airlines: Home of the Limboliner.

EURYDICE. Do you have a goddamn seat on a goddamn flight to goddamn Tampa.

ATTENDANT. Yes, we do happen to have a seat, on the all-new luxury 787 Limboliner.

EURYDICE. Thank God.

ATTENDANT. But that flight has been delayed indefinitely due to turbulence and flatulence.

EURYDICE. Oh, this is hell.

ATTENDANT. No, this is Limbo. For Hell, you must go to Pluto Airlines at Terminal Z, and board the River Styx Puddle Jumper. The equipment is very old, and the airline is experiencing interminable delays. But Captain Charon and the capable Styx flight crew will eventually get you safely to Hell, or wherever your final destination may be. Until your flight is called, however, feel free to wait as long as necessary in Limbo's comfortable departure lounge, where time, we assure you, will pass very very slowly.

(Slow fade on **EURYDICE** *in total despair, crying "Help!!!")*

A CLOSET FLUNG WIDE OPE'

By Shawn Sturnick

CHARACTERS

Son
Mom
Dad

TIME AND PLACE

Today. A suburban kitchen.

A NOTE ABOUT PERFORMANCE

Initially, the text should be spoken so as to conceal the meter and rhyme. Its form should be revealed only gradually.

(**MOM** *irons.* **SON** *enters.*)

SON. Mom, I need to tell you. I'm sure you know it.
    This isn't easy. Mom, I'm – I'm a poet.

MOM. You're what?

SON.   I'm a poet. There I said it.

MOM. You're not a poet.

SON. Mom, give me credit
    For knowing what I am and what I'm not.
    I'm a poet. And for a while I thought
    I could keep it from you. I was afraid
    You wouldn't understand. So I delayed
    In saying what I know I should have said.
    I'm a poet. What's going through your head?

MOM. It's a phase.

SON.   It's not a phase. It's my life.

MOM. Why would you choose –

SON.   You think I'd choose this strife?
    Growing up a poet wasn't easy.
    I felt alone, depressed and sleazy.
    I didn't even know there was a name
    For that which, as a child, was my shame.
    Oh, how those cruel children would tease and shout
    If I ever let a simile slip out.
    I was never comfortable among those
    Who moved so fluidly in this world of prose.
    I thought I suffered from a curse
    And tried to speak, like others, in blank verse;
    Since people thought that same poetry degenerate
    That I would so secretly venerate.
    I felt like some sort of refugee,

And hid myself away in the library.
I'd sneak into the poetry aisle
With an eager but embarrassed smile
And a desire I thought unique to me;
Hoping that no one I knew would see.
Until one rainy Saturday, I met
A man whose impact I shall ne'er forget.
I'd slunk into the stacks to get a fix.
I needed something quick, some limericks.
Instead I found a man whose steady bearing
Demonstrated he was beyond caring
What those other straightforward "Prosers" thought.
Without concern to who was in earshot
He began a dialogue, asking me
Whom I preferred in this realm of poetry.
I couldn't speak, my hands were trembling.
The pieces of my past were reassembling
Themselves into a startling, new world-view.
Oh, could it be that there were others who
Shared my secret and reviled passion,
Yet carried themselves in the same fashion
Akin to this proud and upstanding fellow!
At once I felt a great desire to bellow
"I'm a poet too!" Not caring who heard,
I longed to shout my passion for the word.
But it was a library, so I restrained
From singing of the joy my heart contained.
We spoke of Chaucer –

MOM.   Please!

SON.   No, you need to hear
    And understand that there is naught to fear
    From these men. Chaucer, Spencer, Milton, Pope!
    I rushed headlong down that slippery slope!
    We'd barely started Wordsworth when a chime

Signaled us the library's closing time.
And so we promised once again to meet
Within those stacks. At last I felt complete!
I spent such blissful days beside this man
When something strange and wonderful began
To happen. Other young men wandered by,
And with a lingering look would catch my eye.
A few, overhearing our conversation,
Would join us for a fleeting assignation
Wherein we sampled such temptuous treats
As Tennyson, Byron and Johnny Keats.
My solitary aisle had become
A sort of poetry symposium.
A meeting ground where such like minded men
Could satisfy their each poetic yen.
There we'd engage in –

MOM.   I don't want to know!

SON. Conversation. Once, I dared to show
To those assembled there my own attempt
At poetry. I could not have dreamt
Their critiques! Supportive and insightful;
So well-intentioned; never spiteful.
And thus was born a small poetic haven
Where we welcomed and embraced the language maven.
By word of mouth, young poets found their way,
And once arrived they often chose to stay.
Once, a timid girl approached the stacks, frowning,
In search of some Elizabeth Barret Browning.

MOM. But didn't all that poetry offend her?

SON. Poetry appeals to either gender.

MOM. But how can you be sure that you're...that way?

SON. Mom, poetry is in my DNA.
I love the rhythm, accents, cadence, form.
These hightened elements are to me the norm.
But if some concrete proof is what you seek,

Who else uses rhyming couplets when they speak?
I'm a poet, Mother, a poet proud.
And now I'm not afraid to shout aloud!
I know your shock will pass, and then you'll see
While I may be a poet, I'm still me.

MOM. It's not what any mother wants to hear.

SON. That may be true, but it won't disappear.

MOM. It's just that I'm concerned for your well being.

SON. I know you are. And there's no guaranteeing
That some illiterate, who's full of hate,
Will not some night attempt to perpetrate
A violent crime, committed in haste,
All because of my literary taste.
But the alternative's living a lie.
And that's not a choice I can justify.
I'm a poet Mom. I'll make no excuse.

MOM. Do you think it all began with Dr. Seuss?

SON. That's the spirit, Mom!

MOM.   Well, when in Rome.

SON. Mom, you're the best.

MOM.   I love you too.

DAD.   I'm home.

MOM. Oh my god, your father! You mustn't tell him.

SON. You really think the news would so repel him?

(enter **DAD***)*

DAD. Well, hey sport! Here's an unexpected perk.

SON. Hi, Dad. I'm a poet. How was work?

DAD. You're what?

SON.   I'm a poet.

DAD.   What's he mean?

SON. I mean just what I said.

MOM.   Don't make a scene.

SON. I'm a poet.

DAD. Not in my house you're not.

SON. I'm a poet wherever. What've you got
   against poetry?

DAD. It's just wrong, that's all.

SON. Oh come on, Dad, that thinking is so small.

DAD. Stop that.

SON. Stop what?

DAD. Stop all that rhyming talk.

SON. I can't.

MOM. Honey, let's go for a walk.

DAD. And you're doing it too! What's going on!?

SON. The ugly duckling has become a swan!

DAD. And what the hell is that supposed to mean?

SON. It's a metaphor. You're gonna burst your spleen
   If you don't relax and listen to me.

DAD. All right. I'm listening!

SON. I say to thee
   I'm a poet. No, let me speak.
   I'm a poet. I don't say this to wreak
   havoc on your life. It's simply true.
   And you may not like it, but you can't do
   Anything about it. So why not try
   To listen, to look me in the eye,
   To understand and not be so afraid.
   And let me have this chance to now persuade
   You that your son, whom you were glad to see
   A moment ago is still your son. I'm me.
   The only thing that's changed is now you know
   That I'm a poet. I'd better go.

DAD. You stay right there. Is this some kind of joke?

SON. No. Were you not listening when I spoke?

DAD. Now you stop that. You're doing it again.

SON. I made a rhyme?

DAD. Yes.

SON.   Did I really? When?

DAD. Just then! Stop it. Don't make another rhyme.

SON. Ok, super, from now on I'll just

(**SON** *makes miming motions.*)

MOM.   Mime.

DAD. Tell me why you're doing this to me.

SON. It's simple, Dad. I just love poetry.
     I have been invited to a party
     With T.S. Eliot, Yeats, and Hardy!

DAD. Who the hell are they? Are they coming here?
     I don't want poets in this house.

SON.   That's clear.
     But you've got no clue who poets really are.
     Poets live next door. They hang out at the bar.
     Poets are manly. Poets have endurance.
     Look at Wallace Stephens, seller of insurance.
     William Carlos Williams, poet – M.D.
     Churchill was a poet. Though some would disagree.
     And hold your breath, I've even heard reports
     Of poets playing professional sports.
     Face it Dad, poetry is here to stay.
     And I'm dragging you right into the fray.
     I'm a poet. The fact's not suppressible.
     So why not start with something accessible.
     This is for you. Don't fret about the cost.
     It's a good place to start. It's Robert Frost.

(*Exit* **SON,** *hands* **DAD** *a small book.*)

MOM. Oh, Honey, he's our son. We've got to try.

(**DAD** *reads.*)

DAD. "Two roads diverged in a wood, and I-
     I took the one less traveled by,
     And that has made all the difference."

(*Lights fade.*)

MAN'S BEST FRIEND

By Steven Maistros

CHARACTERS

Coleman

Nelson

The Boston Theatre Marathon production of *MAN'S BEST FRIEND* was directed by Robert Seaver and included:

COLEMAN .... Tony Johnson

NELSON . . . . Chris Silva

(Lights up on two men, a simple table and two chairs. The background is not visible in the darkness. **NELSON** *sits at the table reading from a handful of papers.* **COLEMAN** *paces back and forth nervously. Occasionally he stops and anxiously watches* **NELSON** *read.* **NELSON** *is oblivious of* **COLEMAN** *as he reads. This pacing and reading goes on for an uncomfortably long time and just as it looks like* **COLEMAN** *is going to explode...he does.)*

COLEMAN. *(rambling in one long nervous run on sentence)* I've just got to tell you again that I really appreciate this story exchange, Nelson...and I want you to be objective yet tough...or tough yet objective...you can decide... it's just so good to get some kind of feedback on this type of thing because I sit there in my apartment and I write and I write and my brain is being *(searches for a word)* plundered by Vikings masquerading as questions like "Is this any good?," "Will anyone care?," and... and..."WHY?" and there's no way of knowing if it is any good because you need a reader and I appreciate you being that reader because without you it would be *(pause)* unread.

*(**NELSON** does not acknowledge any of this.* **COLEMAN** *wrings his hands and stares at* **NELSON** *for another shorter uncomfortable length of time.)*

COLEMAN. *(bursting into the rambling again)* I know the Viking analogy was stupid but you get the point, you're just just left there and in a vacuum with no feedback because there's *(pause)*...no...*(pause)* feedback in a vacuum.

*(**COLEMAN** stares again for a shorter length of time.)*

COLEMAN. *(more rambling)* Is it an analogy or a metaphor or a parable or a...well it just sucked, didn't it? Vikings *(laughs)* where'd I think that up? And the feedback in a vacuum thing wasn't too great either. I should just let you read...

NELSON. *(reacting to something in the story)* Hmmm...

> (**COLEMAN** *is startled and stops rambling. His hands start to shake.*)

COLEMAN. *(paranoid)* What is it?

NELSON. *(looking up from the pages as if he's just now noticing* **COLEMAN***)* Pardon?

COLEMAN. What is it?

NELSON. What is what?

COLEMAN. You said...um..."Hmmm"...what did you...

NELSON. I said um?

COLEMAN. No...no...I said "um." You said "Hmmm."

NELSON. Did I?

COLEMAN. Yes, you did. What is it?

NELSON. Oh, just *(fat pause)* something.

COLEMAN. *(even more paranoid)* What something? You haven't even finished the first page and you've found something wrong? Is it the phone call? It's not believable, is it? I had doubts about whether the conversation was believable when I was...

NELSON. *(confused)* The phone call?

COLEMAN. Yes, the phone call Alice gets while she...

NELSON. I don't think I've gotten that far yet. It was something else.

COLEMAN. *(panicked)* What something else? If you haven't got to the phone call then you haven't even read half way down the first page. You've already found something wrong?

NELSON. Listen Coleman, you asked me to be objective yet tough. Are those not your exact words?

COLEMAN. Yes, that's what I want you to be...objective yet... it's my description of the kitchen, isn't it?

NELSON. You've got to calm down. I'm trying to give your story an honest reading, but to do that I've got to put myself into the shoes of Everyreader.

COLEMAN. Everyreader? What are you talking about?

NELSON. Everyreader is the common man. I've got to get into that guy's head and read the story through his eyes.

COLEMAN. You do? I didn't realize this was so complicated.

NELSON. It is complicated. I can't read this as the educated intellectual that I am. I've got to read this as someone who works 9 to 5, who eats a brown bag lunch, who thinks the articles in the sports section are great writing, who comes home from work battered and bruised by...reality. This is an empty cog of the engine that is society. That's who's opinion you want, Coleman.

COLEMAN. *(beginning to freak out again)* And the empty cog has found something wrong with the first page of my story. I worked on the opening page all night and...

NELSON. *(interrupting)* Now don't go having an aneurysm on me. It's just one little problem so far. It's not the end of the world, you know.

COLEMAN. *(another rambling sentence)* I'm sorry...it's...it's just that I've poured my heart and soul into this and I felt like I really made some progress with this story and it's hard to know that the Vikings are ready to pounce on it and *(pause)* pillage.

NELSON. Vikings?

COLEMAN. *(shakes his head)* See...words aren't...

NELSON. *(interrupting)* Listen, you asked me to be tough.

COLEMAN. I know...I know. Thank you for doing this for me. I can handle constructive criticism because that's what I wanted. *(takes a deep breath)* What did you have a problem with?

NELSON. *(doesn't skip a beat)* The title.

COLEMAN. *(looking like he's been punched in the gut)* You haven't even got past the title?

NELSON. Well, it...

COLEMAN. *(really freaking out now)* You've been reading for five minutes and that whole time you were stuck on the title! The very first words at the top of the page are so putrid that you couldn't get past them! *(leans on table)* I've got to lie down.

NELSON. I wouldn't say putrid *(pause)* necessarily. It just doesn't feel right, Coleman. Just listen. *(looks at the page and reads)* "Alice Laughed Again."

(There is a long pause as **NELSON** *sits and ponders the title and Coleman looks on in shock.)*

NELSON. Do you see what I mean?

COLEMAN. What...what do you...mean?

NELSON. It just doesn't dance, does it?

COLEMAN. *(confused)* It doesn't dance?

NELSON. No it...just lies there like a beached whale. What I mean is...and remember that I'm Everyreader here...

COLEMAN. *(getting a hold of himself and eager to get some constructive advice)* O.K. I understand. Be tough and objective.

NELSON. I've just gotten home from the plant.

COLEMAN. *(confused again)* The plant?

NELSON. *(ignoring* **COLEMAN** *and going on)* There's talk of a strike at the plant and management is threatening layoffs.

COLEMAN. *(really confused)* O.K. Wait...did I give you the right story?

NELSON. *(in his own little world)* The wife tells me that little Billy has been sent home from school again for selling crack to kindergartners.

COLEMAN. *(grasping what* **NELSON** *is talking about)* O.K. This is Everyreader's life. I see. You've got other things on your mind. *(pauses and then looks confused again)* Wait... selling crack to kindergartners?

NELSON. There's trouble with my daughter Sally as well. She's been turning tricks for a local motorcycle gang.

COLEMAN. This is quite a family this Everyreader has.

NELSON. And things just aren't the same between the wife and I since I lost my manhood in a freak work related accident.
(There's a pause as **NELSON** *is lost in his little world and* **COLEMAN** *waits for some sense to come of this).*
Last night I had a sexual fantasy about the dog.

COLEMAN. *(yelling)* What the hell are you talking about?

NELSON. *(exacerbated, drops the story to the table)* You don't appreciate my help, do you Coleman?

COLEMAN. Again, I ask what the hell *(pauses and struggles to compose himself)* ...where did the thing about the dog come from?

NELSON. You can get anybody to read your story for you, but I'm giving you more, you see? I'm creating the mindset of the Everyreader. I'm looking at this from his point of view, Coleman. He's the one you've got to reach and these are the realities that he is faced with.

COLEMAN. It seems like this guy has too much on his mind to be doing a lot of reading.

NELSON *(standing up, excited)* Exactly! You see now. Everyreader's mind is heavy with his own sickening reality. *(picking up the pages)* and he picks up your story. He's looking for escape from the daily atrocity that is his life. He needs you to save him, Coleman! So he reads the title *(pauses, then reads)* "Alice Laughed Again" *(long pause after which NELSON drops the pages to the table)* ... and he drops your story. Because it didn't make him forget the pain.

(**NELSON** *dramatically sits down and lets what he has said sink in.*)

COLEMAN. *(yelling)* He's having fantasies about the family dog! I don't think he's going to forget that anytime soon.

NELSON. Coleman...

COLEMAN. *(interrupting)* Or that thing about his daughter and the motor cycle gang.

NELSON. ...if the title dances he'll forget and he'll be enticed into the reality that you're trying to sell.

COLEMAN. But..."it doesn't dance"... what does that mean?

NELSON. *(dramatically)* Torn Asunder the Heart Grows Together.

COLEMAN. What?

NELSON. Torn Asunder the Heart Grows Together... it's the title of a story I wrote.

COLEMAN. And...that dances?

NELSON. *(proudly)* It grabs you, doesn't it?

COLEMAN. But...what does it mean?

NELSON. What doesn't it mean, Coleman? What doesn't it mean?

COLEMAN. Is there a history of insanity in your family?

NELSON. *(ignoring him)* Don't you see how a title like that dances? It engages the mind like a riddle.

COLEMAN. Because it doesn't make any sense?

NELSON. The Darkness Shall Show More Than It Hides. That's another one of mine.

COLEMAN. But my story is about...

NELSON. Coleman, a good title is not about the true meaning of the story. It has to do with engaging the mind. Underneath is Often Also Above. The Bird Flies To Mock Me. All of these are titles that I've used.

COLEMAN. Really?

NELSON. Let's try something. I want you to relax and let your muse speak through you. Close your eyes.

COLEMAN. I really don't think that this will help.

NELSON. Close your eyes.

COLEMAN. *(reluctantly)* All right...all right.

NELSON. Your muse is going to provide you with the title of the your story. You've just got to clear your mind and let it happen. Think of the imponderable and ancient paradoxes.

COLEMAN. I thought I was supposed to be clearing my mind not thinking about imponderable...whatevers...

NELSON. Do both.

COLEMAN. But...

NELSON. Just let it happen. Let the muse give you the title.

*(There is a long pause as **COLEMAN** stands with eyes closed.)*

NELSON. Now tell me. What's coming to you?

COLEMAN. All I can think about is the poor guy with no penis and a slut for a daughter.

NELSON. *(annoyed)* Well, Everyreader isn't going to keep reading with a title like, "Alice Laughed Again." I hate to say this, but your story is a failure.

COLEMAN. *(shocked)* But you haven't even read the whole thing.

NELSON. And I see no reason to. The title hasn't inspired me to continue. I think you really need to rethink the whole thing. I'd consider burning it if I were you.

COLEMAN. But you haven't even read any of it.

NELSON. Don't be too discouraged. I can see an extremely marginal writer inside of you trying to emerge.

COLEMAN. Extremely marginal?

NELSON. But I don't want to candy coat my criticism. It will take a lot of practice.

COLEMAN. Candy coat?

NELSON. Years and years and years and years of practice. But if you haven't given up after this *(pause)* train wreck of a story then you must have the patience to continue.

(NELSON hands COLEMAN the pages. COLEMAN stands there staring at the story in total shock.)

NELSON. *(picks up his bag)* Well, I'm glad I could help you. I've decided that I won't give you a story of mine to read after all. You seem a little *(pause)* below my level, but keep trying. I've got a writing workshop to get to and I haven't read the story for today.

(NELSON pulls a pack of papers from his bag and looks at the front page.)

NELSON. *(reads aloud)* "Under the Stars"

(shakes his head in disgust, to COLEMAN)

This won't take long.

(NELSON walks offstage and COLEMAN watches him for a second and then calls out...)

COLEMAN. Wait a minute!!! Nelson!

(But **NELSON** *is gone.* **COLEMAN** *sits down and stares at the story.)*

COLEMAN. *(to himself)* Where did the Kindergartners get the money to buy crack?

(Lights down.)

THE END

FOR THE TEAM

By Dean O'Donnell

CHARACTERS

BERT . . . . 30s, preferably somewhat overweight
DON . . . . 30s, also somewhat overweight
MELISSA 20s
ROY 20s
VOICE OF UMPIRE

AUTHOR'S NOTE

Please feel free to change player's names and accompanying insults as the Red Sox roster changes. Feel free to change the locations to local locations, the team to your local team, and the players to your local players, except the Yankees.

FOR THE TEAM was first produced at the Boston Theatre Marathon on April 13th, 2003. It was produced by Centastage and directed by Darren Evans. The cast was as follows:

BERT . . . . Jason Beals
DON . . . . Chris Wagner
MELISSA . . . . Stacy Fischer
ROY . . . . .Alexander Albregts
VOICE OF UMPIRE . . . . Ian Sterling

(*SCENE: The bleachers at Fenway Park.*)

(*AT RISE:* **BERT** *and* **DON** *sit behind* **MELISSA** *and* **ROY**. *Actually, they don't sit at all, because the seats in the bleachers are too narrow to fit their asses without some squeezing, so they mostly stand, or perch on the armrests.* **MELISSA** *and* **ROY** *are still dressed in their business clothes, having come to this night game immediately from work.* **BERT** *and* **DON** *are wearing battered, dirty, sweat stained Sox hats, have two beers each, and a bag of peanuts between them.*)

BERT. He's getting tired.

DON. He'll be fine.

BERT. You try and pitch six innings, see how your arm feels.

DON. Don't believe everything you see in the movies. (*to the field:*) These are trained athletes.

BERT. I'm tellin' ya, he's getting' tired!

ROY. Do you mind? We're trying to watch the game here.

BERT. Well excuuuu-uuuuse me.

DON. Are we interferin' with your concentration?

BERT. Whole lotta concentratin' to figure out what's going on while the inning is changin'.

MELISSA. Look, we don't want any trouble here.

BERT. No trouble. No trouble at all.

ROY. We just want to watch the game.

DON. Hey man, watch the game. G'head.

ROY. Thanks.

BERT. So if we can CONTINUE our DISCUSSION, in my considered OPINION, he's going to choke out there in... (*checks his watch*) ...about four minutes.

DON. (*tossing peanut shells on* **ROY** *and* **MELISSA** *for emphasis*) I respectfully DISAGREE. He's got some GAS left in the old ARM, and I BELIEVE that even if he gets himself into a JAM, he'll be able to pitch himself out of it.

ROY. STOP IT!!

BERT. Excuse me?

DON. I'm sorry. Has our disagreement disturbed your day out at the park?

UMP. *(off)* Ball!

ROY. *(controlling himself)* We just want to watch the game. We would appreciate it if you stopped yelling at us –

DON. I'm sorry, was I yelling at you? I thought I was yelling at this gasbag over here.

ROY. We don't want any trouble. You guys have been drinking and you're maybe a little loud. That's all I was saying.

BERT. So you think we're big, drunk, loudmouthed assholes?

ROY. That's not what I said.

DON. But that's what you meant.

UMP. *(off)* Ball!

ROY. No.

BERT. You wanna piece of me?

ROY. No!

DON. You start callin' us names, you better be ready to back it up.

BERT. You think we're gonna let you get away with talkin' that kinda shit to us?

UMP. *(off)* Ball!

MELISSA. WE DON'T WANT ANY TROUBLE! Besides, if he does get into a jam, they'll just take him out. They've got Embree warming up in the bullpen already.

BERT. *(smiling and yelling at the bullpen)* Hey! Spaghetti arm! You think you're going to save the day?

DON. Oh sure, as soon as a pitcher gets in a little trouble, just replace him!

MELISSA. Well, that's why they have so many pitchers, isn't it?

DON. Well, yeah, but they don't have to treat them like... *(to the field:)* ...MUTANTS! There's no FAITH in baseball today.

UMP. *(off)* Ball! Take your base!

BERT. Did I tell you or did I tell you? He's a mess! That arm is like a piece of cement. Nothing left!

MELISSA. But isn't that a good thing? More pitchers mean more guys in the majors, which means more chances for a really good one to show up.

ROY. Uh, honey?

DON. But they don't give anyone a chance! You get a little tired, they take you out. Unless you're Pedro Martinez, you show the least sign of weakness and you're gone.

ROY. Honey?

DON. Excuse me here, we're havin' a conversation.

BERT. You win as many MVP's and Cy Young's as Pedro and you can pitch yourself out of a jam too. Until you do, stop whinin'.

MELISSA. But you make them pitch all nine innings and they blow out their arms quicker, their careers are shorter –

ROY. Honey?

MELISSA. WHAT?

ROY. *(sotto voce)* I can't believe you're talking to these guys.

BERT. OH MY GOD!! He hit him! Did you see that!

DON. What? What?

BERT. *(pointing to the big screen)* Check out the replay! *(**THEY** all watch, and wince simultaneously.)* OOOOH! That had to hurt! *(looking back down at the field)* And there's a conference on the mound.

DON. *(to **MELISSA**:)* See, this is what's wrong with major league baseball. Yeah, he's having a problem, yeah, he hit a guy, but they don't need to take him out.

MELISSA. He's done. You keep him in, he's going to hurt himself and anyone who comes to the plate.

ROY. *(to **MELISSA**:)* You shouldn't argue with these guys.

DON. He needs five minutes to rest and get his head together.

BERT. Dude, five minutes might just do it. Look, they're stalling up there.

DON. You can't have a five-minute mound conference.

BERT. Where've you been? There's no rushing in baseball.

DON. He's fightin' to stay in the game, he just needs some time to himself.

MELISSA. They're going to take him out.

DON. If the game were somehow delayed.

BERT. Game on! And they're leaving him in! YOU MORON! WHAT ARE YOU THINKING!

DON. Say. Say a fan ran on the field.

BERT. You nuts?

MELISSA. I'm not hearing this.

DON. I've never thought clearer in my life. Say a fan ran on the field, they have to stop the game until the field is clear.

ROY. It's a minimum two hundred and fifty dollar fine and the night in jail.

BERT. You're kiddin'.

ROY. Nope. Says so in the program. *(holds up the program)*

DON. It's worth it.

MELISSA. To keep him in the game? You're nuts.

DON. How many times have you been sitting, watching a game and you wanna be a part of it? Isn't that why we come to the park? Yer sittin' at home, you yell at the TV, ya feel like a nutbag. At least if you're here there's a chance the ump is gonna hear you call him a shit for brains, right?

BERT. Yellin' at the ump is one thing, but –

DON. But this is our chance to become part of the history of major league baseball. How many times have you said that you'd give anything for a spot in the playoffs?

BERT. Too many.

DON. Well what are ya willing ta give? Huh?

ROY. It's a misdemeanor.

DON. Shut up! Bert, man, ya gotta listen to me. This is where we separate the fans from the bums. If spending a night in jail would get the Sox into the playoffs, wouldja do it?

BERT. I guess.

DON. Don't guess! Know!

MELISSA. It's only April.

DON. The pitches decide the play. The plays decide the inning. The innings decide the game, and the games decide the playoffs. I'm tellin' ya Bert, this next ten minutes could decide the fate of the entire season.

UMP. *(off)* Ball!

DON. The clock is really tickin' here. This is our chance. What are ya willin' to do? What'll you do for the team?

BERT. But there's no sayin' that if we do this we'll win.

DON. There ain't no guarantees in life, either. The best you can do is take your shot and let the chips fall.

ROY. I think this would be considered conspiracy to commit a crime.

MELISSA. Oh, shut up, Roy.

DON. We can make history. We can be right up there with the Babe, and Yaz, and Ted Williams.

BERT. With Yaz?

DON. Well maybe not Yaz, but we'll be an asterisk in sports history. Next to the score for this game, and down the bottom of the page it'll say, "Game delayed by fans on the field."

BERT. An asterisk?

DON. Like Roger Maris.

BERT. They got rid of that.

UMP. *(off)* Ball!

DON. I can't wait for ya anymore, Bert. He walks this one and they'll probably pull him. If you're gonna do it, wait till they get me, then start yer run. (**DON** *rips open his shirt to display a huge red and blue "B" painted on his chest and stomach.*) I was savin' this for an Ortiz grand slam, but I can't think of a better time than right now. (**DON** *removes his shirt and throws it on the chair, to* **MELISSA**.) It was nice meetin' ya.

MELISSA. Good luck!

(MELISSA *shakes his hand. It is a strangely touching moment.* DON *takes a deep breath, and runs off, screaming at the top of his lungs. The others follow his progress around the field with their eyes.*)

ROY. Well, he's delayed the game.

BERT. That man is a true fan.

MELISSA. *(to the pitcher)* Take the time! Rest your arm!

(THEY *watch, their heads moving in unison, as* DON *runs around the field.* THEY *all wince together as he's caught.*)

ROY. Oh, that's gotta hurt!

MELISSA. Do they really need to twist his arms like that?

BERT. Ah hell, that was, what? Barely three minutes?

ROY. More like two and a half.

BERT. I ain't gonna let Don go down by himself.

(BERT *rips open his shirt to display the Red Sox logo painted on his chest and belly.*)

MELISSA. Wow, that's good. Did you do that yourself?

BERT. My wife. She's good with the paints. Very artistic.

MELISSA. Tell her I thought it was very good.

BERT. You betcha. Do me a favor?

MELISSA. Anything for a true fan.

BERT. Call her and tell her where we are. I'm in the book. In Medford. Bert Dumphy.

MELISSA. I will.

BERT. Here I go!

(BERT *runs off screaming.* THEY *follow his progress.*)

ROY. Actually this is a good plan. Half of the security team is still dealing with the first guy.

MELISSA. His name is Don.

ROY. Whatever.

MELISSA. Not whatever. Their names were Don and Bert, they were Red Sox fans, and they will be remembered.

ROY. Don't you think you're taking this a little too seriously?

MELISSA. What would you do, Roy? What would you do for the team?

ROY. Are you kidding? It's just baseball.

MELISSA. *(shocked pause)* I guess I have my answer then. *(sighs)* Roy, it was a nice date. I'd appreciate it if you come and bail us out, but if you don't, I'll understand.

ROY. Wait! What do you –

MELISSA. Don and Bert had their hearts in the right place, but they were slow. I figure I can avoid security for at least a minute more than they could.

ROY. You're not going to.

MELISSA. *(She kisses him on the cheek.)* Yes I am. I'm going to make a run for it.

ROY. No, I thought you might rip your shirt open.

MELISSA. Y'know what? I think I will.

> (**MELISSA** *rips her shirt open, underneath is an old, tattered Red Sox tank top, obviously a size or so too small.*)

My dad bought it for me when I was fifteen, and the Sox have never lost one when I wore it to the park.

ROY. But –

MELISSA. You can take the girl out of Southie, but you'll never take Southie out of the girl.

> (**MELISSA** *runs off screaming.* **ROY** *follows her progress, finally winces, sits down and starts eating Cracker Jack. The lights fade.*)

UMP. *(off)* Steeeeeeeee-rike!

> *(Curtain.)*

SO FINE DINING

By Zachary L. Shrier

CHARACTERS

Umberto

Ernie

(Lights up on the foyer of a chic Italian restaurant, "Sant'Ambrogio." It's afternoon and all patrons have left. The founder and master chef, **UMBERTO BACCHUS,** *35, a native New Yorker, hurries to clear a table. He resets it with only a white tablecloth, no flatware.)*

(Enter **ERNIE GOLDHABER,** *26, recent graduate of cooking school, carrying a manila folder. Tentative.)*

UMBERTO. Ernie?

ERNIE. *(somewhat scared)* Yes...?

UMBERTO. Welcome welcome welcome. *(spreading his arms)* Sant'Ambrogio. Come in! Come in!

ERNIE. I'm here for the interview. Are you...Chef Bacchus?

UMBERTO. Oh, golly! Will you *please* call me Umberto.

ERNIE. Umberto?

UMBERTO. It's more than possible that we're going to be colleagues, Ernie.

ERNIE. Okay.

UMBERTO. *(straightens the tablecloth)* I know, some chefs are so adamant about preserving that power differential with their staff. I tell my students, the more power a chef arrogates to himself – the less power remains for the food.

ERNIE. That's funny.

*(***UMBERTO*** raises an eyebrow.)*

No, I mean...I didn't mean funny. I meant interesting.

UMBERTO. You can think it's funny, too. That's *all right.*

ERNIE. Just the idea that...of competing with your own food.

UMBERTO. But it's true. The chef should create, and disappear. Never should he mistake himself for the *point* of the art.

ERNIE. Hmm.

UMBERTO. The only thing that matters is the food.

ERNIE. Just food?

UMBERTO. That's right. Just food.

(The two men stand a moment, checking each other out across the table.)

Why don't we have a seat?

(They sit.)

ERNIE. *(looking around)* Your trattoria is beautiful. You got such nice reviews.

UMBERTO. Thank you, Ernie. I'm trying to create a special context here. Do you understand what I mean by *context?*

ERNIE. I think so.

UMBERTO. What do you imagine I mean?

ERNIE. Well, a context...a kind of place for something...

UMBERTO. A set of circumstances.

ERNIE. Circumstances?

UMBERTO. Yes. Circumstances in which an event occurs.

ERNIE. Dining.

UMBERTO. At least you didn't say, *eating.* Yes, dining, I suppose. Although that seems a preposterously modest goal. Dining can occur at a delicatessen, Ernie. At a pizzeria. It doesn't really require a *context.*

ERNIE. That's really interesting.

UMBERTO. *(tapping his index finger against his temple)* My patrons think *dining,* but I want *us* to really think about something much more...ambitious.

ERNIE. A context.

UMBERTO. Exactly. A context for a relationship of sorts. A seduction.

ERNIE. Sed... ?

UMBERTO. A seduction of the human mind and palate, that's right. Using tastes, textures, smells. That I create.

(long pause)

So. Your resume said you're a graduate of the Apicus Academy in Florence, did it not?

(ERNIE *opens his folder and fumbles through a bunch of photocopied pages, pulling out two.)*

ERNIE. Um…well… actually I did my Associates Degree at New England ulinary Institute. But I did spend some of spring semester last year studying Tuscan cuisine at Apicus. And I received a certificate in Classical Food Preparation.

UMBERTO. Degrees mean nothing to me. Talk to me about food.

ERNIE. Like, what I've prepared?

UMBERTO. If you like.

ERNIE. Okay. Hmm, well, I've prepared over 10,000 meals in the course of my curriculum…

UMBERTO. Jesus, that makes you sound like a burger outlet.

ERNIE. Pardon?

UMBERTO. Those large numbers. They actually detract from your appeal to me. Somewhat.

ERNIE. I'm sorry.

UMBERTO. No, it's fine. Just don't give me *data*.

ERNIE. I'm sorry, I don't understand…

UMBERTO. Give me an experience. Something you made… something you tasted. I want *details*. Make me *feel* it with my mouth.

ERNIE. Okay. Hmm.

(ponders a second)

Okay, well, when I was in Italy last year, we took this day trip to a bakery in Volterra, and they taught us how to make *bombolone*. It's like an Italian donut.

UMBERTO. I know.

ERNIE. Right, of course. Okay.

UMBERTO. Go on.

(As **ERNIE** *speaks,* **UMBERTO** *closes his eyes and clearly enjoys.)*

ERNIE. So, that was pretty cool. I sort of varied the recipe a little and added these semi-sweet chocolate shavings. In the shape of little curls.

(Pause. **UMBERTO** *'s eyes still closed.)*

And I used a sweet marscapone cheese as the filling instead of the usual cream.

(Pause. **UMBERTO** *'s eyes flip open.)*

UMBERTO. *(frustrated)* That's it?

ERNIE. Huh?

UMBERTO. Don't stop, for God's sake. Keep talking to me.

ERNIE. About what?

UMBERTO. About *what?* About your bombolone. About the sweet cheese. About those cute chocolate curly-q's. Or anything else. Just *don't stop.*

ERNIE. Okay.

UMBERTO. And don't make it all sound so horribly mundane, either.

ERNIE. I'm sorry.

UMBERTO. Shush. Make it come alive, Ernie. C'mon. Thrill me. *Go.*

ERNIE. Well there *was* this pasta alla Bottarga that you could get down on Santo Spirto that was absolutely delicious. I've been working for the last few months to try and reverse-engineer the recipe.

UMBERTO. *(whispering)* Details.

ERNIE. Okay. The pasta was a very heavy farfalle made with extra egg yolk.

UMBERTO. How heavy?

ERNIE. Oh, *very* heavy. Yellow and dense and…moist.

UMBERTO. Ohh. That's nice.

ERNIE. Yeah. Like each bowtie had its own weight and identity. You'd want to eat them one at a time. Bite each one slowly, you know?

UMBERTO. God. What about the sauce?

ERNIE. The sauce was salty, with these gorgeous, tender fish roe that pop very gently between your teeth. But the base was a heavy cream – like a crème fraîche – flavored with boiled heirloom grape tomatoes and pickled capers.

UMBERTO. *(hissing)* I could help you make that.

ERNIE. Really?

UMBERTO. Oh yeah.

ERNIE. But that was only the Primi. Wait until you hear about the main course!

UMBERTO. *Feed me.*

ERNIE. A grilled baby lamb, served very rare…

UMBERTO. Still pink inside?

ERNIE. Totally. And exceptionally juicy. Cut into two-inch cubes. Roasted medium carrots and fresh rosemary…

UMBERTO. Two-inch *cubes?*

ERNIE. Yeah.

UMBERTO. No! Skip this one. Move on.

ERNIE. Uh…

UMBERTO. Move on! Move on!

ERNIE. Okay, we did this session on braised beef at this place, Tavola Toscana…

UMBERTO. I know it well…

ERNIE. Do you? Near Santa Maria Novella?

UMBERTO. Shut up and get to the braised beef.

ERNIE. Right. Fresh gingerroot, each piece about the size of a quarter, boiled together with cinnamon, orange zest, anise, garden fennel, and whiskey, the beef shanks at a bare simmer – the hot liquid converging around it..

UMBERTO. *(fanning himself with his spread fingers)* I can taste it.

ERNIE. Each piece was so tender, Umberto, a 3-month-old infant could chew it in his gums. It would fall apart if you kissed it with your lips.

UMBERTO. *(grabbing the tablecloth with both fists)* Did you kiss it, Ernie?

ERNIE. Just enough to suck the gravy out of the beef strands.

UMBERTO. Ogggghhhhhh! I would have *soiled* myself!

ERNIE. I needed a two-hour nap after I'd finished it.

UMBERTO. Give me dessert, Ernesto!

ERNIE. *(breathing heavily)* Okay, are you ready for this?

UMBERTO. Yes!

ERNIE. Sure?

UMBERTO. Stop teasing you little shit!

ERNIE. We're sitting there, waiting – *begging* for dessert after this braised beef from the afterlife. And I'm thinking, how are they going to finish this meal? I'm picturing gelato – maybe a nocciola or a pistacio or a blackberry –

UMBERTO. No! A zabaglione tart with marsala-lemon sauce!

ERNIE. Not even close!

UMBERTO. Arrggh! What in Christ's name was it??

ERNIE. Flan!

UMBERTO. Flan?

ERNIE. It looked like this beautiful mint flan, but I couldn't tell. There was a chocolate-dipped leaf on the plate, apricot sauce drizzled everywhere, glistening in the candlelight...

UMBERTO. Did you lick it?

ERNIE. I took my tiny dessert spoon, and dipped it so gently into the flan and took this tender, shivering sliver of the flan to my lips. And I sucked it, ever so tenderly, through my lips. And it glazed my tongue and melted inside my hot mouth. And that's when it hit me...

UMBERTO. No... .

ERNIE. Yes!

UMBERTO. No, they didn't! Those horny little Italians!

ERNIE. Basil! It was a *BASIL FLAN!*

UMBERTO. And the chocolate-dipped leaf?

ERNIE. BASIL!

(**UMBERTO** *expels a huge rush of air, lurching forward onto the table.*)

UMBERTO. How did that make you feel, Ernie??

ERNIE. Umberto…I wanted to cup that basil flan in my hands… .

UMBERTO. Say it… !

ERNIE. And I wanted to place it on the tips of my fingers…

UMBERTO. Say it! Sing it out… .!

ERNIE. And *shove it up my ass!*

UMBERTO. YES! YES!

ERNIE. I wanted to fuck that flan with every sinew of my body!

UMBERTO. Did you do it, Ernie? Did you fuck that flan?

ERNIE. No. Everyone was standing around. My whole class. My professors.

UMBERTO. They don't understand food.

ERNIE. They don't understand anything.

(*Long pause. Both men are breathing heavily.*)

UMBERTO. Can I tell you something, Ernie.

ERNIE. Anything, boss.

UMBERTO. I think I may have the recipe for that flan some-where.

ERNIE. And the ingredients?

UMBERTO. Every one.

ERNIE. And the time?

UMBERTO. We don't open for 3 hours.

ERNIE. Shall we?

(**UMBERTO** *launches himself off of his chair, crawls across the table, and straddles* **ERNIE**'*s chair, collapsing in his embrace.*)

(*The men begin kissing hungrily.*)

(*Curtain.*)

GRIP

By Kirsten Greenidge

CHARACTERS

BERNICE. . . . . 80s, African-American
HELEN. . . . . 80s, African-American

SETTING

A city bus, the present.

(a city bus)

(BERNICE *and* **HELEN** *sit.)*

BERNICE. "*Welcome* to Ryle's jazz lounge."

HELEN. Jazz?: *no, no, no.*

BERNICE. It's like cake: it's like pie.

HELEN. Be careful around me.

BERNICE. Jazz: tastes: good.

HELEN. May be. But then you got them Jazzy girls: bare legs, bare shoulders. It's not right, not right.

BERNICE. That was then. This is now: this will be cake. Pie.

(pause)

I do like me my cake. And pie. If I still had teeth: I could have some.

HELEN. You've already had more than some. That's why you have no teeth now.

BERNICE. You're wrong.

HELEN. We're heading in an easterly direction.

BERNICE. I don't have teeth because I'm old.

HELEN. We're headed in a loop.

BERNICE. Where are you going?

HELEN. I haven't decided yet.

BERNICE. Ryles jazz lounge.

HELEN. No. No jazz. None at all. We're going easterly, in a loop, and we're going where I say so get used to it.

BERNICE. Ryles –

HELEN. You hold onto things and you don't let go. You have a vice grip.

BERNICE. I don't have a vice grip. I have *no* grip. They make sure of that. They strap me in. By my wrists to my bed. They use my ankles, too.

HELEN. But I always undo you. I help you out. And that's when I see it, this strong grip, this vice grip.

BERNICE. I do hold onto Woolworth rhinestones. I remember those. I hold onto them something fierce.

HELEN. I hold onto rotary telephones. It took work to make a telephone call way back when. You appreciated the connection. You appreciated the voice at the other end of the line.

BERNICE. Rhinestones aren't always trashy.

HELEN. Eighty-six those rhinestones. Think of something better. Like Hashed Browns. The old fashioned kind.

BERNICE. With grits?

HELEN. No.

BERNICE. Then blech.

HELEN. That sound produces more water than you need in your mouth.

BERNICE. Blech, blech: I'm always thirsty. I can always use more water.

HELEN. It's cold outside. Your throat might freeze over. If you leaned your head back you could kill yourself with the chill: a pond of ice in your throat makes for quite a chill. I'd have to defrost it. I always help you, in one way or another. Chill in your bones, in the air: freezed up throat. But I'd break the ice.

BERNICE. We're on our bus where it's warm. I don't need help.

HELEN. Later.

(slight pause)

BERNICE. I miss Woolworths'.

HELEN. Now there're the Walmarts.

BERNICE. Welcome to Walmart.

HELEN. Now there're the Targets.

BERNICE. No one welcomes you at Target.

(pause)

And there's nothing but plastic in those Walmarts. Blech. Not a rhinestone in sight.

HELEN. Maybe.

BERNICE. Not the good kind. There's a good kind and a bad kind. Walmart has the kind that Woolworth's would never even put on the shelf.

HELEN. Hot dogs. They have hot dogs at Walmart. And popcorn. It's like the circus. That's another thing I hold onto. A good circus. The tent kind. The kind that came with a side show and people they kept in dark places because they're too freakish for the light. I miss a good circus. Even if we only got to go on that only day for us, I appreciated a good circus way back when. I appreciated a hot dog and some fresh popped corn.

BERNICE. No good to me. I have no teeth.

HELEN. Easterly, don't you worry: you'll get all you want soon.

BERNICE. I hope.

HELEN. Yes, yes, yes.

BERNICE. We won't just loop and loop until we're found will we?

HELEN. Not this time. This time fortune has winked our way. This time she has nodded in our direction. Our easterly direction. The way of the wind.

BERNICE. Usually it's back to our beds.

HELEN. They don't strap *me* in.

BERNICE. Maybe this time they'll realize they should.

HELEN. I'd fight them. I'd fight them to the finish. I *must* walk: my ankles need to know that their job isn't done yet; they've still got to hold me up.

BERNICE. My straps have buckles. I can't undo buckles. My fingers can't feel them the right way: they can't slip the buckle loose the right way. Straps hurt more than you think. I have bruises. Black and purple.

HELEN. See how you've got that grip? That vice grip? We're on our bus now, let all that strap business go. We're headed easterly on our loop, remember something better.

BERNICE. Rhinestones can look special even when they're old.

(pause)

I tell my daughter not to worry. She sees the bruises and she cries. She doesn't bring her kids anymore. They didn't cry. Just stared.

(pause)

I used to push her around in a carriage. A blue one with big white wheels and openings on the sides for her to see out of. And panels to put over the openings when I wanted to hide her from nosy people on the street because people really take to brown babies. It's when we're too old, when the sap's dried that makes people frown. Or worse. Smile with sugar that burns, that really means: look at the cute old-lady.

(pause)

Real metal spokes on those wheels, though.

(pause)

Now she sees me strapped to my bed. I have no panels so I can't hide.

HELEN. My kids bring fried chicken. From Kentucky Fried Chicken, not even homemade. It's a big party when they come. I'm the only one not invited. I have to be there, since *they* came to see *me*. I can't walk away.

BERNICE. You could.

HELEN. I'd hurt their feelings. They might walk out and never come back and some fried chicken is better than no fried chicken.

BERNICE. Or they might not pay your bill on purpose. Then you'll get strapped like me. Then we'd never get out.

HELEN. There shouldn't be such a fuss about us getting out. Who cares. Less work for everyone in the long run. In the great scope of things.

(pause)

BERNICE. Decided where you're going?

HELEN. (*closes her eyes*) Swimming pool.

BERNICE. Napping in the sun?

HELEN. Snorkeling in the blue.

BERNICE. There's nothing to see in a pool.

HELEN. I go deep underneath all that blue.

BERNICE. No plants. No fish.

HELEN. Only blue, the way I like it. My ankles just have to help my feet flutter. They don't have to hold me up. The weight of me doesn't tell me I'm alive, all the blue does.

BERNICE. Where is this pool?

HELEN. Baltimore, Maryland.

BERNICE. You've held onto that pool.

HELEN. I haven't.

BERNICE. For all these years you've held onto it.

HELEN. Not with a grip, though. I don't hold it so tight I can't think of anything else or anywhere else I want to go.

BERNICE. You with your pool. Holding on. Gripping.

HELEN. It's better than rhinestones. That's all *you've* got.

BERNICE. And that carriage. With the panels and the metal spokes – carriages don't have metal spokes anymore – and my little brown baby. And Ryles. From before my babies. From before when I could dance and drink like a fish and was more me than ever I was or would be.

HELEN. Jazz. Vice grip: I'm right.

BERNICE. Well, what else do *you* have, Ms. Snippity-Snip?

HELEN. North pole.

BERNICE. Doesn't count. You've never been.

HELEN. I could have.

BERNICE. Name another.

HELEN. Chicken coop.

BERNICE. Too smelly.

HELEN. Hens are warm. Keep the chill from settling.

BERNICE. Good idea, then.

HELEN. Now you.

BERNICE. My old sidewalk. All the houses had stoops.

HELEN. That sidewalk does not count. You bring it up too often. Name something else.

BERNICE. It's too hard to remember.

HELEN. Because of your tight grip on those rhinestones, on that Woolworth's.

BERNICE. What if, what if we both had a tight grip?

HELEN. Dead. The both of us I've already told you. We'd have no reason to pretend we have someplace to go, no reason to break out for our easterly bus ride. We'd die. Kaput. We'd be over. You in your bed with your straps.

BERNICE. You with your heavy body.

HELEN. Gets heavier by the day.

BERNICE. Maybe we could hold onto something else, something brand new, shiny different, the two of us.

HELEN. I like snorkeling. I like those hens.

BERNICE. It might be better than waiting. For rhinestones and metal spokes.

HELEN. And rotary phones.

BERNICE. Yes.

HELEN. Do you mean we should get off our bus?

BERNICE. We're always found because we always stay on. They can always cart us back. Let's use the next stop.

HELEN. It's cold outside.

BERNICE. There are no more Woolworths.

HELEN. If your throat freezes I won't be able to do anything. Mine will freeze, too. Our last bits of sap will ice over and that will be the end of both of us.

BERNICE. There are no more rhinestones and that's all I want in the whole world.

HELEN. (*as the bus slows for the next stop*) Ponds of ice. No way to melt them.

(The bus stops.)

BERNICE. You have store bought chicken. I have bruises.

(She stands. She exits the bus. She stands on the curb as **HELEN** *watches.* **BERNICE** *waves as she leans her head back and her mouth open. The door to the bus closes and the bus lurches forward.)*

HELEN. (*to the driver:*) Wait.

(The bus stops short and the door opens.)

(**HELEN** *exits. She goes to* **BERNICE**. *She leans her head back and opens her mouth. The bus continues on.)*

End of Play.

SEX EDUCATION

By Jerry Bisantz

CHARACTERS

Dan
Linda
Jim
Ben

The Boston Theatre Marathon production of *SEX EDUCATION* was directed by Nancy Curran and included:

DAN . . . . Barlow Adamson
LINDA . . . . Michelle Aguillon
JIM . . . . Matthew Leavis
BEN . . . . Nick Andrews

*(**SETTING**: The play takes place in the parents' bed-room. There is a door upstage right, a chest of drawers on the right back wall and a bed downstage left. Upstage left is a door to a closet. It is 11 a.m. on a school day, the early 1980s.)*

*(**AT RISE**: BEN and JIM, two best friends, aged 12 years-old, enter the bedroom. They are each carrying a beer and are extremely nervous.)*

JIM. *(flipping on the light)* Come on…it's all right!

BEN. Just a few minutes, OK?

JIM. You think your old man is hiding underneath the bed? *(He rushes to bed, gets down on his knees.)* Come on out, Mr. Silverman!

BEN. That's not funny…

JIM. Oh…it's a little funny…*(takes a swig of beer)* Come on, yer not even drinkin'.

BEN. It's warm.

JIM. Of course it's warm. You think my old man wouldn't know if we stole one of his cold ones? Besides, he drinks so much 'a this stuff he loses count.

*(**JIM** flops on the bed.)*

BEN. Don't do that! You'll mess up the bed…My mom knows exactly how she makes it!

JIM. You know, Ben, yer a real wimp!

BEN. Just cause *your* mom wouldn't give a shit if she caught you skippin' school…

JIM. She cares…just don't get caught.

BEN. *(carefully taking a sip of his beer)* Uuughh…God! Yer father drinks the worst piss in the world!

JIM. He gets it by the truck-full. I don't think he really gives a shit what it tastes like. Long as it gets us high! *(takes a slug)*

BEN. *(looking around nervously)* Look…can we go into another room? Maybe the rec room or something?

JIM. *(swings his legs around and sits up)* Oh, no way, man! You told me we were gonna see 'em! Don't chicken out on me now, man! *(starts to make "chicken" noises)*

BEN. All right…one look, but can we go in a few minutes? I'm getting weirded out in here.

JIM. Come on, Ben! It's yer parent's bedroom! *(smooths his hands over the covers)* Ooohhh…just think of all the action these sheets have seen! Maybe baby Ben started out here! *(starts to fake a baby's cry)*

BEN. Cut it out!!

JIM. You know, you have the hottest mom in the neighborhood!

BEN. Shut up about my mom!!

JIM. OK, OK…I'm kidding! Jesus, Ben, take it easy…*(He slugs some more beer.)* Look…I'll go over it one more time.

BEN. …You don't have to…

JIM. No, I will!! Because yer really freaking out here. And your voice gets all high like that jerk in the BeeGees so I'll tell you once more… #1: No one knows we are here. #2: We are supposed to be in school. #3: Yer mom's at work, #4: Yer dad's at work, #5: we are here for a reason, so stop stalling!

BEN. Alright. One look, but then we have to go.

JIM. I promise. Cross my heart and swear to die.

BEN. *(goes to closet door, opens it up and starts to feel around under clothing)* Yeah, you swear all right.

JIM. Do you need any help?

BEN. I know where they are. *(We hear him moving items around.)* SHIT!!!

JIM. WHAT???

BEN. THEY'RE NOT HERE!!!

JIM. AAAHH, CHRIST!! I KNEW YOU LIED!!!

BEN. *(turns around with a box in his hand; chuckling)* Fooled ya…*(walks over to the bed with the box)*

JIM. You dork!

BEN. *(holding the lid over the box)* Are you ready for a trip to heaven?

JIM. X rated?

BEN. TRIPLE X!!! *(Does the "Space Odyssey" Song: he uncovers the box and pulls out a "Penthouse" magazine.)* BA DA!!!

JIM. WOW!!! September 1978. That was a good year, right?

BEN. You think they have bad years? *(He opens the pages.)*

JIM. Go to the fold-out…

BEN. *(riffling through the pages)* There are no fold outs in Penthouse. It ain't as classy as Playboy.

JIM. Yeah but…whoa!! Look at that!! Oh my God! Their showing…

BEN. EVERYTHING, buddy, EVERYTHING!

JIM. WOW!!!!! *(There is a moment of profound reverence as they ogle the pages.* **JIM** *points at the magazine)* How come she has blonde hair but she's black down here?.

BEN. She's not a "natural"…

JIM. You mean she dyes her hair down there?

BEN. *(incredulous look)* Yeah, Jim, she dyed her hair DOWN THERE…

JIM. …whoa…look at the size of those…

BEN. Nice, huh?

JIM. *(turns page; points)* Oh my God! Look at that…you can see the whole…

BEN. I KNOW! I heard my Dad talking about this guy that owns this magazine. Bob Gutzy–ony…anyway, my Dad told his friend that this guy is crazy. He'll show ANYTHING!!

JIM. It's just…I mean it's…weird looking, isn't it? It's so…I wonder what it feels like… ?

BEN. *(interrupting)* Danny McCoy told me.

JIM. *You* know Danny McCoy?

BEN. I'm his paper boy. Sometimes when I come to collect he's home alone. We shoot the shit.

JIM. He's cool.

BEN. He's always stoned. Anyways, he told me he had sex with Donna Karinsky...all the way, too!

JIM. She's a dog!

BEN. Yeah, well, forget the face.

JIM. *(closes his eyes)* I'm trying to...it's impossible!

BEN. Well, she has a great set on her and she wears those tight hip huggers...anyways, I asked him what it, you know, what it *felt* like...down there...

JIM. What'd he say?

BEN. He said it feels like a wet balloon!

JIM. Yuck!!!

BEN. Yeah, a wet balloon...and he said it gets *really* wet...

JIM. Maybe she peed on him!

BEN. *(laughing)* Yeah!! She peed on him! I'll bet she did!

JIM. *(pause)* You know who'd get real wet? Farrah Fawcett.

BEN. Huh?

JIM. Fawcett...get it... ?

BEN. Oh...Yeah, real funny...but I bet the real Farrah Fawcett doesn't have to do this for some money...

JIM. Do you think they get a lot of money for this?

BEN. I certainly hope so! *(pause as he turns page)* I wonder if this one went to Catholic school?

JIM. My mom said they do it for the drugs.

BEN. They have moms and brothers and sisters...Hey! what would you do if we saw your sister in here?

JIM. Which one?

BEN. Jenny.

JIM. I'd kill her. *(pause)* Or, I'd make her give me half her money to shut my mouth.

(They turn the page again.)

BEN. Whoa! Look at that one.

JIM. Best so far...She's so pretty...

(They are mesmerized. We hear the sound of a slamming door. And keys turning.)

BEN. SHIT!!! *(takes the magazine, throws it in the box)*

JIM. Who is it?

BEN. *(runs to the window and looks out)* Holy shit, it's my Dad. If he finds us we're dead! Hurry up!

JIM. What do we do?

BEN. Hide under the bed! Hurry up! I'll hide in the closet! He probably just left something in the house!

*(They scramble to their respective "posts." **BEN** takes the box of mags with him; we hear the sounds of two voices, one male and one female.)*

DAN. *(offstage voice)* Watch your step…

LINDA. *(offstage)* I've climbed stairs before, ya know…

*(The door swings open and **DAN** enters. **DANIEL SILVER-MAN** is mid 40s, dressed in a suit, carrying a bottle of wine that is half empty. He has his arm around **LINDA**, a 30-ish woman dressed in casual business attire.)*

DAN. Yes! But you never climbed *my* stairs before! *(He roughly scoops her in his arms and kisses her)*

LINDA. You're gonna spill the wine all over the rug!

DAN. …and we wouldn't want that now, would we? *(kisses her again)*

LINDA. *(pulling away and looking around)* Nice place. I've never been in this part of town before. *(looks around)* Very nice. Your wife must have good taste…

DAN. Yes…she has good taste. And can we *please* not bring her up right now?

LINDA. Hey, this was your idea not mine…I was perfectly happy in Saugus.

DAN. *(walks over to her, starts to remove her top)* We don't have time to drive all the way there.

LINDA. Slow down a second, Danny…Pour me some of that wine.

DAN. Fine… *(pours some wine into one of the glasses he brought)* It's pretty good stuff. From Portugal…

LINDA. It's wine. Don't pretend to be some wine connoisseur. It'll get me high, that's all I care. *(She takes wine, sits on bed; drinks.)*

DAN. *(walks towards her)* I know how to make you high, *Ms.* Stapleton…*(He kisses her again; begins to play with her bra.)*

LINDA. *(pulls away)* Let's get under the covers. It's freezing in here…

DAN. *(suddenly upset)* NO! I mean…let's not get under the covers, OK?

LINDA. Whattaya mean?

DAN. Can we just stay on top of the bed? That's…OK with you, isn't it?

LINDA. What're you, scared? Listen, Danny, you're the one who insisted on coming over here. If you're freaked out by it let's just go back to the office and call the whole day off.

(DAN gets up and paces around. There is a pause as he considers her suggestion.)

DAN. No…I…I want you. *(walks over to her; on his knees in front of her)* I want you…here. Now.

LINDA. But, *not* inside the covers?

DAN. …is that OK?

LINDA. *(considering)* No, it's not OK…but I guess it'll have to do. *(She kisses him)* It's a good thing you have a great ass! *(They kiss again,* **DAN** *falls gently on top of her, his hand sliding up her leg.)* mmm…Cold.

DAN. What?

LINDA. Cold…I said I'm cold.

DAN. How can you be so cold when I'm so hot for you…

LINDA. Listen, Romeo, I'm freezing. Just get something to put over us…

DAN. *(rolls off her, perturbed)* Fine! I'll get something…

(DAN walks to the closet and opens the door. Neither the audience or **LINDA** *can see* **BEN** *hiding in the closet. All we can see is* **DAN**'s *face as he sees his son. An audible gasp comes out of* **DAN.** *He stares at the door about to say something. He is frozen.* **BEN,** *unseen and terrified, burrows deeper into the closet, trying to escape into a hole of his own making.)*

LINDA. *(calling from the bed)* Did ya find something? *(pause)* Danny? What is it? Come on, I'm freezing my ass off here...

DAN. *(inaudibly at first, as HE continues to stare into the closet)* Out.

LINDA. What? Honey, what did you say?

DAN. *(louder)* Out! *(turns around)* Out! OUT!! GET OUT OF MY ROOM!!! PLEASE! GET OUT, NOW!!!

LINDA. *(stands up, struggles with her blouse)* Danny, what's wrong? What the hell happened?

DAN. Get the hell out of my bedroom!!!

LINDA. *(points at him)* One second you're...

DAN. GET OUT OF MY HOUSE!!!

LINDA. You're nuts! You know that? You're certifiably crazy ass-nuts!

DAN. JUST GO!!! *(HE starts to push her out)*

LINDA. *(turns on him)* Oh, I'll go allright. I should've listened to Chris! You're crazy! And you better stay the hell away from me, or I swear I'll make some phone calls that'll get you in **SO** much trouble... *(goes to door)*

DAN. GOODBYE*!!!*

*(**LINDA** slams the door, he leans against it, shaking. **DAN** looks at the closet door as we hear the sounds of **LINDA**'s footsteps running down the stairs and a door slamming. There is nothing but quiet, **DAN** locked to his position at the bedroom door, **BEN** staying in the closet. **DAN** slowly walks towards the door. He is in the center of the room, facing the door. He gathers himself; speaks in a low, resigned voice.)*

DAN. Ben...your...your mother and I...umm...you see, we... *(clears his throat)* it's hard to explain to a kid... . *(clears his throat)* Oh, Jesus, Ben, I'm just so sorry...

*(**DAN** runs to the door, wildly opens it and runs out. There is no movement for a good five seconds. Slowly, **JIM** crawls out from under the bed. **HE** walks over to the closet door.)*

JIM. Ben? Ben? Are you alright?

BEN. *(from closet)* Leave me alone!

JIM. No!

> *(There is a long pause.)*

BEN. Leave me alone, OK?

JIM. No, I won't leave you alone. *(pause)* Come on, ya can't stay in that closet forever. *(pause)*

BEN. Wanna bet... ?

JIM. *(trying to cheer him)* Come on, it'll...your...your father won't do that again...it was all just a bad screw up...

BEN. Don't talk about my father!

JIM. He's just...he just did something stupid is all.

BEN. I said shut up about my father!

JIM. OK, fine...*(long pause)* Come on, Ben. You can't stay there all day.

BEN. Watch me.

JIM. Fine. I'll just sit here then...*(sits in middle of floor)*

BEN. Go. I don't want you staying here.

JIM. *(stands)* Not unless you get out of that closet.

BEN. I'm not getting out with you here.

JIM. Fine. Then you're not leaving. *(sits again)*

BEN. *(long pause; then)* Jim, I know you wanna help. I'm fine, OK? I just gotta think...

JIM. I don't want...

BEN. *(interrupting)* I'll call ya tonight. I promise. I'll call.

JIM. *(thinks about it)* Yeah, OK.

BEN. I'm sorry...

JIM. S'long as you call me. *(He gets up.)*

BEN. I'm OK, really. I just...I gotta think, OK?

JIM. *(after a pause)* OK...*(walks towards the door)* Hey...call me...

BEN. Wait!

> **(JIM** *turns at the door. The box of magazines slides on the floor from the closet, landing right at* **JIM***'s feet.)*

JIM. *(He has struck gold)* Whoa…

BEN. Keep 'em. I don't want 'em anymore.

JIM. Are you sure?

BEN. Take 'em.

JIM. Won't you get into trouble?

BEN. Take 'em!

JIM. …cause we can split 'em up…

BEN. I don't want them anymore!

JIM. OK, if you don't want 'em. *(He picks up the box.)*

BEN. I'll call you tonight. I promise.

JIM. Thanks, Ben. Sorry about yer Dad.

BEN. Yeah.

JIM. My Dad's a jerk too, ya know.

BEN. I know.

JIM. Bye.

> (**JIM** *exits with the box in his arms. There is a long pause.* **BEN** *slowly walks out of the closet as the lights fade to black.*)

> *(Blackout.)*

CLAIRE DANES POSTER

By Tom Berry

CHARACTERS

TIM, a man in his late 20's, early 30's

JOSH, his friend, also late 20's, early 30's

CLAIRE DANES POSTER was given its world premiere at Boston Theater Marathon V on April 13, 2003 at Boston Playwrights' Theatre (Kate Snodgrass – artistic director). The play was produced by Boston Theatre Works (Jason Southerland – artistic director) and was directed by Nancy Curran Willis. The cast included:

TIM. . . . . Tom Lawlor

JOSH . . . . Jason Yaitanes

(The lights come up on a small room, starkly furnished. There is a cot with a small table beside it. The table is cluttered with 8 or 9 bottles of Zima, mostly empty, with some of the empties placed back in a cardboard six-pack holder. There is also a chair in the room with a suit coat and tie draped over the back of it. A poster of actress Claire Danes hangs slightly askew on the wall above the cot. TIM, dressed in an unbuttoned white shirt and dark suit pants, sits on the cot staring at the poster, taking swigs from one of the Zima bottles. He appears solemn and contemplative.)

(A couple of quick knocks on the door. JOSH enters. He is also dressed in a dark suit.)

JOSH. Hey man, you almost ready to go to the funer–? *(Sees that he is not fully dressed)* Oh, sorry. I can come back in a minute.

(TIM stands, as if he's been caught doing something wrong.)

TIM. No, I'm all set.

(JOSH stands near the door, waiting. He notices the empty Zima bottles on the table.)

JOSH. Oh. Dude. I'll just come back when you're –

TIM. Hey, I'm fine.

JOSH. You sure?

TIM. *(pointedly)* Yes. *(beat)* I'm fine.

JOSH. *(hesitating)* I know you must be in a really bad place right now. I mean, you're drinking *Zima.*

(They stand silent for a beat.)

JOSH. I can go stall if you want.

TIM. *(distantly)* No, I'm ready.

(TIM sits down on the cot again and looks at the poster.)

JOSH. *(after a pause)* We don't want to be late.

TIM. *(staring at the poster, as if in a trance)* Uh huh.

JOSH. *(after an uncomfortable silence)* Can I ask a dumb question?

TIM. *(matter-of-factly)* Wouldn't be the first time.

JOSH. *(acknowledging* **TIM***'s sarcasm)* Ha ha. Good one. *(beat)* Who's the chick?

TIM. *(looking at* **JOSH***, coming out of the trance)* Claire Danes. *(looking at poster, back into the trance)* Isn't she great?

JOSH. Yeah. *(pause, then laughs)* A Great Dane. *(stops laughing, clears throat, then after an uncomfortable pause)* So, who the hell is Claire Danes?

TIM. You ever see the movie "Romeo & Juliet?"

> (**JOSH** *shakes his head no.*)

TIM. "The Rainmaker?"

> (**JOSH** *shakes his head again, with a slight grimace.*)

TIM. "Little Women?"

> (**JOSH** *gives him the "are you kidding me?" look.*)

TIM. Right. No. *(pauses)* The chick from "My So Called Life?"

JOSH. Nope. Whatever. Why do you have a poster of her?

TIM. She was sent to me.

JOSH. *(sarcastically)* Did you buy "Little Women" on DVD or something?

> (**TIM** *glares at* **JOSH***.*)

JOSH. Sorry.

TIM. Forget it. You wouldn't understand.

JOSH. What's to understand about a poster?

TIM. Never mind. You'll laugh anyway.

JOSH. I won't laugh.

TIM. You always do.

JOSH. Well, I might laugh just a little.

TIM. Forget it then.

JOSH. Aw, come on. Tell me. *(pause)* Alright, alright, alright. I *promise* I won't laugh.

(**TIM** *looks at* **JOSH** *for a beat, then at the poster, beat.*)

TIM. Look at her eyes.

JOSH. *(skeptically)* Oh.........kay.

TIM. What do you see?

JOSH. *(looks, bewildered, then answers, reluctantly)* Is this a trick question?

TIM. *(frustrated)* Dude.

JOSH. OK. OK. *(looks at poster)* Umm. *(searching for an answer)* Hmm. *(pauses to think)* They're...green?

TIM. *(a bit impatient)* Yeah. But look closer. Really *look*.

(**JOSH** *studies poster more intently for a moment, contorting his face in a painfully, constipated stare.*)

JOSH. Am I supposed to see like a boat or something?

TIM. *(beat)* You're a dick.

JOSH. I'm not trying to be a dick. I just don't see what's so great about some poster of –

TIM. Claire Danes.

JOSH. Right. Claire Danes. I mean, what's the big deal?

TIM. *(with growing exasperation)* Remember when we were in college, and you couldn't understand why I wanted to go out with the woman that lived down the hall from us? You said, "I don't see what the hell is so great about her. I'd get bored with her in about five minutes." You remember that?

JOSH. I said that?

TIM. *(nods)* Yeah. You said she was plain looking. That she was "plainer than plain."

JOSH. Oh, yeah, her. What was her name again?

TIM. Jane. *(slight beat)* But that's not the point.

JOSH. The point, right. *(beat)* What is the point?

TIM. The point is you didn't see what I saw.

JOSH. If I could do that, I'd be clairvoyant. But, I'm not. *(quick beat)* Heh. Heh. Claire Danes. Clair-voyant.

(another quick beat. **TIM** *glares at* **JOSH***)* I'm just not getting the whole fascination with this poster of Claire Danes. I mean, there are hundreds of 90-pound Hollywood waifs that are ten times hotter than her.

TIM. You've got to look past the fact that it's Claire Danes. It's got nothing to do with that.

JOSH. You lost me, Timmy.

TIM. It's what she represents.

JOSH. Your so called life?

TIM. *(looks back at poster)* In a way, yes. It's like she's –*(notices out of the corner of his eye that* **JOSH** *is smirking)* Laugh and you're a dead man.

*(***JOSH** *puts his hands up.)*

TIM. Like she's watching over me. She sees all. She is the eyes of Dr. T.J. Eckelburg.

JOSH. That cop show with Shatner and Adrian Zmed?

TIM. Jesus, you don't know who Claire Danes is, but you remember Adrian Zmed? No. T.J. *Eckel*burg. The Great Gatsby?

JOSH. I hated that book.

TIM. The giant billboard that overlooked the scene of the accident where Myrtle was killed...

JOSH. Lord of the Flies – now there's a book.

TIM. ...The symbolic, omniscient presence that knows and sees all.

JOSH. *(pauses)* Isn't that redundant? Being omniscient and knowing and seeing all?

TIM. You know what I mean.

JOSH. Yes, the definition of omniscient is about the only thing I've been able to follow so far. But what the hell does this have to do with Claire Danes!?

TIM. *(pause, looks dreamily at poster)* She sees me. Really sees me...and I see her.

JOSH. *(picking up Zima bottle)* Wow. This stuff really packs a punch. What proof is this shit?

TIM. I'm not drunk, man. *(pauses, his last attempt to explain)* I went to Suzy's favorite coffee shop this morning. I ordered her usual drink – a vanilla latte. I hate vanilla lattes, but I ordered it anyway, and I sat there for a while. When I was coming out of the shop – there's this movie rental place next door – I saw this poster. It stopped me dead in my tracks. I stood there for an hour, just staring at this poster. I couldn't bring myself to walk away. So, I bought it. I had to. Especially for today. To see her again. For her to see me. *(beat)* I need her to see me. *(He pauses, trying desperately to hold his composure. He starts again, his voice shaky, almost whispered)* I need her to see me.

JOSH. *(suddenly Josh gets it)* Oh, my God. She does have Suzy's eyes. Man, I'm sorry. Really, I...

(He falls silent.)

*(The two men stare at the poster in knowing silence for a moment. Suddenly, **JOSH** goes to the poster, takes out the bottom two tacks, folds the poster and tries to cover up the mouth area of the face on the poster.)*

TIM. What're you doing?

JOSH. Covering her mouth.

TIM. Why?

JOSH. Her mouth reminds me of my ex, with that little – *(He imitates the mouth to demonstrate his point)*. You see it?

TIM. *(looks)* Huh. You're right. I didn't notice that before. I was too busy –

JOSH. – looking at the eyes, yeah I know. *(pause)* C'mon, Dr. Eckelburg, let's go get through this.

TIM. Yeah. Ok.

*(**JOSH** begins to leave, stops, picks up **TIM**'s tie from the chair and throws it to him.)*

JOSH. I'll go warm up the car.

*(**JOSH** exits.)*

(**TIM** *puts on his tie, staring at the poster as he does this. He grabs the coat from the chair and puts it on. He moves toward the door, stops and turns to look one last time at the poster. He looks at it for a moment, then smiles softly. He sighs.* **TIM** *then moves to the door and silently exits.*)

(*Lights out.*)

INSTANT KARMA

By Susanna Ralli

CHARACTERS

SAM and **DONNA**. . . . . A 30-something couple

INSTANT KARMA was produced at the Perishable Theatre in Providence, Rhode Island. It was directed by Moira Costigan with the following cast:

SAM . . . . Mike LoCicern

DONNA . . . . Karen Carpenter

*(**SCENE:** An empty stage, except for **SAM** at center and a small object several feet in front of him on the floor.)*

*(**AT RISE:** Lights come up to reveal **SAM**, standing with his hand over his mouth. He's dressed casually in jeans and a T-shirt, but stands stiffly, frozen, looking in horror at the floor in front of him. After a few moments, **DONNA** enters from the right. She walks over to join **SAM**, noisily eating potato chips from a small plastic bag. Her rounded stomach reveals that she's about six months pregnant. **DONNA** is dressed in a "power maternity" suit, which has several large pockets on the jacket. During the play, she continuously, ferociously, and ecstatically eats tidbits of food that are stashed in small plastic bags in the pockets of her jacket.)*

DONNA. Hey, did you get the pizza?

*(**DONNA** looks at **SAM** curiously when he doesn't answer, then looks at the floor in the direction in which he's staring. Then she looks back at **SAM**.)*

What?

SAM. He's dead.

DONNA. Who's dead?

*(**DONNA** looks more closely at the floor, then raises her eyebrows when she sees what **SAM** sees. Calmly, she eats another chip. On the floor, in front of **SAM**, is a large, brown mouse. It isn't moving.)*

Wow. That's a big one.

SAM. He's gone, and it's all my fault.

DONNA. What happened?

*(**SAM** clutches his head and moans. As he describes the accident, he painfully re-enacts it.)*

SAM. Oh, God, it was an accident. I didn't mean to. I didn't want to. I just saw him there, next to my foot, and I tried to get out of the way, and instead...instead...

DONNA. You squished him.

SAM. I don't think you understand the karmic implications here.

DONNA. Sure I do. It's tragic. *(pause)* So let's flush it and have dinner.

(Finished with the potato chips, DONNA puts the empty plastic bag in a pocket. From another pocket, she pulls out a chicken drumstick and takes a big bite out of it.)

SAM. Donna, I took a life. A little life, but a soul nonetheless. Every day, *every day* I try to think of ways I can be a good person. To make life a little more pleasant for everyone.

(SAM looks down at his hands.)

And now look at me. I'm evil. I'm unclean. I've murdered one of God's creatures!

DONNA. It's a mouse!

SAM. You look down there and all you see is a disease-ridden rodent. But I see more. I see a beautiful denizen of planet Earth who has been tragically killed. And now I'm going to have to pay the price. I don't know when, I don't know where. But someday...

DONNA. A mouse is going to come up to you, say "Payback time," and shoot you in the toe?

SAM. Don't you feel anything for this poor creature?

DONNA. I'm totally sympathetic. It must have been awful. He's going innocently about his mouse business, when you come along, towering over him, yell "Eek!" and stamp on him.

SAM. I didn't yell "Eek!"

DONNA. I'm sure you didn't, honey.

(Pause. DONNA finishes the chicken drumstick, gnawing on the bone. She puts the chicken bone in a pocket, then takes out a chocolate bar and begins to eat it.)

I was thinking maybe Chinese for dinner. What do you think?

SAM. You aren't taking this seriously, are you? Well I can tell you, it was heartbreaking, when he looked up at me, with those big brown eyes, and that cute paisley bow-tie...

(**DONNA** *looks at* **SAM** *strangely when he says "bow-tie."*)

...and I tripped and my big foot came down right on his tiny little head.

(**SAM** *moves downstage toward the mouse, then kneels down next to it and speaks tenderly.*)

It must be pretty tough, being a mouse. Worrying all the time – Will he find enough to eat? Will he get caught in the electrical wires in the wall? Did he invest enough in his IRA? How long can he stretch his health insurance?

(**SAM** *shudders.* **DONNA** *has stopped eating and is looking at him intensely.*)

And you know what the worst part is. I bet he has a family. Little babies, living in the wall. Waiting for him to come home with a few crumbs of stale bread. He went out to the office, just like any other day. And then Daddy never came home. And they just keep waiting for him. Waiting.

(**DONNA** *looks at* **SAM** *suspiciously.*)

DONNA. Did something happen at work today?

(**SAM** *stands up and looks at* **DONNA**.)

SAM. What do you mean?

DONNA. Isn't your office doing some reshuffling thing?

SAM. Yes.

DONNA. You weren't...They didn't...reshuffle you today, did they?

SAM. No.

DONNA. Thank God.

SAM. They reshuffled John.

DONNA. John?

SAM. John Marino.

DONNA. The guy with five kids John Marino?

SAM. Yes, and all I can think about are those five little mice...

DONNA. Children...

SAM. ...and a sixth on the way. What will they do?

(**DONNA** *reflexively puts her hand over her abdomen.* **SAM** *starts to hyperventilate.*)

They made me do it, Donna. They made me tell John he had to go. And when he was leaving, he smiled at me. I destroyed his life, and he just stood there, squished, smiling at me.

(**SAM** *runs to* **DONNA**'s *side.*)

I don't know what to do! What can I do?!

(**DONNA** *looks at* **SAM** *sympathetically, then seems to make a decision. She pats his hand and exits right. While she's gone,* **SAM** *looks in utter misery at the mouse. A few moments later,* **DONNA** *returns with a shoe-box and plastic gloves, which she firmly hands to* **SAM**. *He nods, takes them solemnly, and puts on the gloves.* **SAM** *goes over to the mouse, picks it up by the tail, and puts it in the shoe-box. Then he takes off the gloves and puts them in the shoe-box too. He puts on the cover. Leaving the shoe-box on the floor,* **SAM** *stands up, closes his eyes, and folds his hands solemnly in front of him.*)

SAM. Dear Lord, we are gathered here today to mourn the loss of this poor mouse.

(**DONNA** *starts to laugh, then pretends to be coughing. Shaking her head, she takes some pretzels out of a pocket and begins to munch on them.*)

He was a good mouse. He didn't bother anybody. He got his quarterly reports in on time. He minded his own business and didn't deserve to...to...

(**DONNA**'s *crunching becomes really loud.* **SAM** *stops speaking and looks back at her. She stops chewing for a moment.*)

Dear Lord, please make our little friend welcome in mouse heaven.

(**DONNA** *bursts out laughing.*)

How can you be so insensitive? I'm carrying a burden here.

(**DONNA** *stops laughing and puts one hand on her belly. When she speaks to* **SAM**, *she's very upset. As she speaks,* **SAM** *watches her with varying degrees of surprise and comprehension.*)

DONNA. Burden? *You're* carrying a burden? I'm carrying an extra fifty pounds of burden. Fifty pounds of hungry burden. All I think about is feeding him – poor little John – feeding him day and night. And when I feel him moving around inside me, and I picture him – with his big brown eyes and his cute little whiskers – I'm so filled with love that I can't stand it. I'm terrified. Everything I eat – everything I think and feel and do – will affect him. Everything I do could mean the difference between health and sickness, wisdom and evil…

SAM. Life and death.

(**DONNA** *pulls the chicken bone and an unopened chocolate bar out of her pockets and holds one in each hand. She gestures with the chocolate when she says "Gandhi." She gestures with the bone when she says "Hitler.")*

DONNA. If I eat chocolate he might be Gandhi. If I eat chicken, he might be who? Hitler? And for God's sake – what happens if I eat cheese doodles?

(**DONNA** *stuffs the bone and chocolate in her pockets and holds her head in her hands.* **SAM** *walks over to* **DONNA** *and puts his arm around her.*)

SAM. You're right, honey. *(He pulls away.)* Damn, I just wish I didn't feel so responsible!

(DONNA grabs SAM's arm and places his hand on her belly.)

DONNA. Feel responsible.

(SAM thinks for a moment. Then he lifts his hand off DONNA's belly and touches her face. They look at each other with great tenderness for a moment. Then SAM picks up the shoe-box.)

SAM. I'll be right back.

(SAM exits right with the shoe-box. DONNA casually looks down on the floor where the mouse had been. Suddenly, staring, she looks devastated.)

DONNA. Oh God. The babies.

(She covers her mouth with her hand, standing in just about the same pose that SAM did in the beginning of the play. In a moment, SAM returns, carrying an opened bag of cheese doodles. Hearing him return, DONNA recovers her composure and lowers her hand. SAM offers her some cheese doodles, and they both take some out of the bag. Looking into each other's eyes, they eat together. Lights fade to black.)

END

ETHICS OF THE PROFESSION

By Paul Kahn

CHARACTERS

Tommy

Doctor Hoffman

The Boston Theatre Marathon production of *ETHICS OF THE PRO-FESSION* included:

TOMMY . . . . Diego Arciniegas

DOCTOR HOFFMAN . . . . Susanne Nitter

(SCENE: A hospital room.)

*(AT RISE: **TOMMY**, a newly injured quadriplegic man sits in a wheelchair, staring blankly out the window. He looks unkempt and is dressed in a combination of hospital pajamas and old sweats. **DOCTOR HOFFMAN** knocks on the open door and enters. She wears a white medical jacket over a colorful dress.)*

DOCTOR. Mr. O'Brien, I'm Joan Hoffman. Can I come in?

TOMMY. Looks like you're already in.

DOCTOR. I was hoping we could talk for a few minutes.

TOMMY. About what?

DOCTOR. I'm with the psychiatric consultation service.

TOMMY. You're a shrink.

DOCTOR. Guilty as charged.

TOMMY. I didn't ask for a shrink. Who sent you?

DOCTOR. Big Brother? I just came to see how you were doing.

TOMMY. I'm fine.

DOCTOR. I hear that you're leaving our tender mercies tomorrow. Looking forward to going home?

TOMMY. Yeah.

DOCTOR. With a few new gadgets, like the wheelchair. How are you doing with that?

TOMMY. Doing okay.

DOCTOR. I just did a stupid thing, didn't I? Committed what we shrinks call avoidance. I said "a few new gadgets," when I really meant the whole scene – your spinal cord injury, your broken neck. Do you find that people do that to you – trivialize?

TOMMY. My mother can't look at me.

DOCTOR. Catholic?

TOMMY. The whole nine yards. What's it to you?

DOCTOR. Just trying to get a picture. You're tougher than that, pride yourself on being tough.

TOMMY. I deal. I look at stuff.

DOCTOR. So, what do you see when you look at yourself?

TOMMY. Doc, I'm not into this.

DOCTOR. You just deal.

TOMMY. That's right.

DOCTOR. Clint Eastwood and Arnold Schwarzenegger all rolled up into one. I apologize, Tommy. Can I call you Tommy? I joke when I'm uncomfortable. And there's no comfortable way of telling someone he's a liar.

TOMMY. Where do you get off –

DOCTOR. *(interrupting)* I don't believe you, Tommy. I don't think you're fine. *(looking out the window)* Great view from up here. The city shines. Can't see the squalor. Tommy, you're an attorney.

TOMMY. I used to be.

DOCTOR. Then let me present my evidence. A guy who was fine, who was looking forward to going home would have made arrangements for how he was going to live with his "few new gadgets." The social service department gave you a referral to the visiting nurses, so you could get home health aides. They also referred you to the independent living center, so you could get hooked up with peer support, find a wheelchair accessible apartment and get eligible for PCAs. But, you haven't followed through on anything. They checked.

TOMMY. So, I'm lazy.

DOCTOR. I don't think so. More like unmotivated. Depressed. That's what the staff who work with you say.

TOMMY. Big Brother's little helpers.

DOCTOR. They're good people, but they can't reach you. They think you're holding a lot inside.

TOMMY. So, they sent you to pry me open.

DOCTOR. I have a modest reputation as a good listener.

TOMMY. Well, Joan – Can I call you Joan? – I'm sorry to waste your time, but they're wrong. Like I said, I'm fine, just fine. Your evidence is inconclusive.

DOCTOR. I have more. Something particularly distressing to the staff. You've had a visitor, several times – Dr. Long. Everybody knows who he is.

TOMMY. A good listener, like you.

DOCTOR. So, you're telling me that Dr. Death was just paying a social call. He wasn't here on business?

TOMMY. I don't owe any explanations to you or those nosy bitches who report to you. Get the hell out of my room. Too bad there's no comfortable way of saying that.

DOCTOR. Are you always so hostile to people who want to help you?

TOMMY. I don't need any help.

DOCTOR. We all need help.

TOMMY. That's so easy for people like you to say, walking around on your two good legs, with your fancy degrees, that you think give you the right to barge into people's rooms and call them liars. What help do *you* need?

DOCTOR. I need you to be truthful with me. Tommy, are you thinking about killing yourself? Did you ask Dr. Long to help you do it?

TOMMY. No! What the hell business is it of yours anyhow?

DOCTOR. Tommy, I've worked with lots of people that have been in your situation. They all get depressed for a while. You've had a terrible accident.

TOMMY. It wasn't an accident. I was drunk.

DOCTOR. You blame yourself. That's common, too. But, people change how they feel.

TOMMY. And live happily ever after?

DOCTOR. No, but they find reasons to believe that, even with a disability, their lives can be worthwhile.

TOMMY. Or, maybe they're too chicken to face the truth – that they'd be better off dead.

DOCTOR. Is that the truth about *you*? Do you really think that you'd be better off dead?

TOMMY. What would you say about a lush who fucked up his job, fucked up his marriage, fucked up his body, fucked up everything that ever meant anything to him?

DOCTOR. I'd say that person had a lot to forgive himself for, but forgiveness was possible.

TOMMY. And I'd say you were full of crap. You shrinks are just like priests, except you charge big bucks to hear confessions. Some slob spills his guts to you. You tell him it's all his mother's fault that he's screwed up. He hands you a hundred, goes out and screws up some more.

DOCTOR. So, I'm pretty worthless, about as worthless as you feel.

TOMMY. Whatever you say.

DOCTOR. No, whatever *you* say. I mean I'm not misinterpreting your intent to demolish me, am I? And, you did it so swiftly and surely. I wouldn't want to go up against you on the witness stand.

TOMMY. Why are you sticking your nose up my ass? What's your game?

DOCTOR. There's no game. I believe that, if I give honesty, I have a better chance of getting honesty in return. That's all. And, I want you to tell me honestly if you're getting into bed with Dr. Long.

TOMMY. What if I said yes?

DOCTOR. I'm supposed to try to stop you. That's the ethic of my profession. Don't give up on the patient, even when he's given up on himself. Hold on to hope, even when he has none. But, when people are in a lot of pain, I sometimes wonder what I'm doing.

TOMMY. In law school they taught us ethics, too. They taught us about justice. All that did was make me feel more cheated when shit happened.

DOCTOR. Better not to have any expectations.

TOMMY. Yeah, better. Dr Long understands that. Everyone else wants something from me – like bravery, or patience, or fucking honesty. He doesn't want anything.

DOCTOR. Just your life.

TOMMY. He can have it. It's garbage. Here's the truth, Joan. Tomorrow when I get discharged I'm meeting Dr. Long at my apartment. I don't give a shit if it isn't wheelchair accessible. The only way I'm getting out is in a body bag. I'm getting out of this whole fucking mess!

DOCTOR. Thank you for your honesty, Tommy. Now I'm going to give you some in return. See how that works. You're not leaving here tomorrow. I'm pink-papering you. You're a danger to yourself. I'm keeping you here for as long as I possibly can.

TOMMY. You can't do that. I'll sue you. I'll have your goddamn license yanked!

DOCTOR. On what grounds? I'd go up against you on this one, Tommy. You just told me your life is garbage. You just told me you were going to kill yourself. I have a duty here. It's the ethic of my profession.

TOMMY. Goddamn you! You conned me. You said you didn't want to see people in pain. Look at me! What else do you see?

DOCTOR. Strength, defiance, possibilities. I know you're in pain now, but I'll help you get through it.

TOMMY. I can't get through it! And, you can't make me try, you bitch! Goddamn fucking sadistic bitch! I'll kill you!

DOCTOR. You can't kill me, if you kill yourself first. Not a great reason to live, but it's a start. At least it's a start.

END

HAPPY DAUGHTER

By Greg Lam

CHARACTERS

Carol

Mother

Boyfriend

Rita

The Boston Theatre Marathon production of *HAPPY DAUGHTER* was directed by Kevin Fennessy. and included:

CAROL . . . . Bernice Sim

MOTHER . . . . Bonnie Lee Whang

BOYFRIEND . . . . Kent French

RITA . . . . Kate Fitz Kelly

*(AT RISE: An empty stool in the middle of a small stage.
CAROL enters. She is an Asian-American woman in her
early to mid-twenties. She is very talky and a bit woozy,
like she's having drinks at the bar. She primarily addresses
the audience directly throughout, not the other characters,
though she may be looking at them from time to time.)*

CAROL. So where was I? What time is it? *(checks watch)* I'm a
little frazzled now. I just got back from taking my parents to the airport. Well, my mother, anyway. Geez. I
mean, this past couple of days...so chaotic. I mean, it
started when my mom came last week to visit... *(sound
of a plane passing overhead)* Why she wanted to come
here to Iowa rather than have me go back to San Fran
is beyond me.

MOTHER. *(from offstage)* What a darling little town!

CAROL. Oh, she was sooo over the top. It was right off the
plane with hugs and "Oh, how pretty you look..."

*(MOTHER rushes onstage, thin but a very strong per-
sonality. She hugs CAROL and speaks at the same time.)*

MOTHER. Oh, how pretty you look. Simply gorgeous, don't
you think so, dear?

CAROL. Oh yes. She brought along her boyfriend. Right.
She has a boyfriend now. She's not supposed to have a
boyfriend. Divorced middle-aged Asian women are not
supposed to have boyfriends, right?

*(The BOYFRIEND enters. He's much younger than the
mother, a little older than CAROL, friendly and gregari-
ous, if a bit tacky. They start to shake hands.)*

BOYFRIEND. Yes, ma'am. I'm glad to meet you Carol. I've
heard so much about you.

CAROL. And Caucasian. Did I mention he's Caucasian? Divorced, middle-aged Asian mothers are not supposed to have cute Caucasian boyfriends who are decades younger than they are. Didn't she get the memo? She's supposed to play mah-jong and go on group vacation tours with her other lonely friends. And didn't she give an evil eye to those white guys I dated in High School?

BOYFRIEND. I'm just so happy to finally meet you! Come here.

(*The* BOYFRIEND *spreads his arms for a bear hug, but the scene freezes as…*)

CAROL. Uh – Next we stopped for drinks on the way to their motel.

(RITA, *a waitress/host dressed in something black and tight, brings on the set for next scene. She smokes constantly. Small table and three chairs. Bad music plays in the background.*)

CAROL. Which, in Iowa, meant Highway 80 Sunnyside Café, conveniently located just off Highway 80.

(RITA *finishes setting table, and speaks in a deadpan monotone.*)

RITA. Welcome to the Highway 80 Sunnyside Café, conveniently located just off Highway 80. My name's Rita. Table for three? Right this way.

(*They sit.* RITA *takes order.*)

CAROL. And I ordered –

MOTHER. A diet Coke with a twist? Come on! It's us. Live it up.

CAROL. And they had –

BOYFRIEND. Two martinis on the rocks.

MOTHER. That's our special drink.

BOYFRIEND. For special occasions like this.

CAROL. They have a special drink? Since when? They've been together for like two seconds.

RITA. Two martinis, rocks, dc with lime. Be right back. (*exits*)

CAROL. I never had a special drink with anyone. What's wrong with me?

(**MOTHER** *hands* **CAROL** *some photos.*)

MOTHER. Carol. I'll show you pictures of our trip to Italy.

CAROL. Italy? Italy! And we talked –

MOTHER. So, darling. How is the writing thing? Are you Amy Tan or Margaret Cho yet?

CAROL. And when that subject passed it was –

MOTHER. How about a boyfriend? When do I see a grandson?

(**RITA** *enters with drinks. Sets them down semi-consciously while the* **BOYFRIEND**'*s eyes wander. Exits.*)

BOYFRIEND. So we were both in Tai Chi class together, right? That's how we met. She was my warmup partner.

CAROL. Isn't that so sweet?

(**CAROL** *rolls her eyes or makes a gagging noise.* **RITA** *enters.*)

RITA. Beer nuts.

(**RITA** *carelessly tosses a tray of nuts on table, exits.*)

BOYFRIEND. Thanks, doll!

(*The* **BOYFRIEND** *starts eating them.*)

CAROL. And then she started talking about him.

MOTHER. Yes. Oh, I know it's sudden in your eyes. You don't think Mom should have a boyfriend. But that's how this type of thing is. Someday you'll feel this way. Wait and see, wait and see.

CAROL. And I was all: Yes, I guess so, I suppose. But Mother was still –

MOTHER. He makes me feel young again. After your father left I was all. But now I feel, you know. Like I can live again.

CAROL. As…as long as you're OK, Mother. As long as you guys are happy, I said. But then the entertainment started. Oh my God, the entertainment…

(**RITA** *enters with microphone. She speaks into it in the same deadpan monotone.*)

RITA. It's Friday night boys and girls. So you know what that means. It's the Okey-Dokey Karoake celebration. And I'm your hostess with the most-est.

CAROL. Kill me now.

RITA. Let's start out with some Cher. Everybody likes Cher, right?

CAROL. They, um, seemed to like it.

MOTHER & BOYFRIEND. *(singing)* "It's in his kiss, that's where it is!"

CAROL. But then afterward Mom's New Boyfriend said –

BOYFRIEND. For an old biddy, that Cher sure has a hot piece of –

CAROL. Moving on. It's best to get past that part quickly.

(*Scene freeze.* **MOTHER** *and the* **BOYFRIEND** *rearrange the chairs to form a car, with the* **BOYFRIEND** *driving,* **MOTHER** *in shotgun, and* **CAROL** *in back.*)

CAROL. After that, we got into the car, and it was on to dinner.

MOTHER. I don't care, we can eat anywhere. Is there Chinese in Iowa?

CAROL. "Mom, WE are the only Chinese in Iowa." Well I didn't actually say that, but I wanted to. Oh, the ride was loads of fun.

MOTHER. Should we stop there?

CAROL. I don't think that's a good idea.

MOTHER. No? Is "Bebe's Exotic Club and Grill" not in the Zagats?

BOYFRIEND. I don't think that's the type of place that's primarily known for its cuisine, hon.

CAROL. But we did finally find a place, though.

(RITA, *the same actress, enters in a slinky Oriental dress. Same deadpan delivery.*)

RITA. Welcome to the Wok of Life, Iowa's finest Chinese/ Polynesian/ Miscellaneous Oriental Cuisine. Table for three? Right this way.

(RITA *carries on the table for three. Exits.*)

CAROL. Everything seemed to be all right at the restaurant, though. They laughed at each other's jokes.

(MOTHER *and the* BOYFRIEND *laugh.*)

CAROL. They held each other's hands.

(MOTHER *and the* BOYFRIEND *hold each other's hand.* RITA *enters with tray of drinks.*)

CAROL. They ordered drinks.

RITA. Scorpion Bowl, Diet Coke, Suffering Bastard. *(exits)*

CAROL. And, of course, they sipped each other's "exotic" cocktails.

(*They sip each other's drink.*)

CAROL. And this, well, this was the strangest thing of all.

(RITA *enters the stage with a microphone.*)

RITA. And so on Friday Night, it's of course time for the Karaoke Kaos Krew. And we have a special request to start things off.

CAROL. I had this sinking feeling in my stomach all of a sudden.

(*The* BOYFRIEND *steps to the microphone.*)

BOYFRIEND. It's a honor to be able to sing this to a very special woman.

MOTHER. He's embarrasing me. Silly man.

(*Music starts. It's a romantic song. He sings shockingly well.*)

BOYFRIEND. *(singing)*

    THE WAY YOU WEAR YOUR HAT
    THE WAY YOU SIP YOUR TEA
    THE MEMORY OF ALL THAT
    NO THEY CAN'T TAKE THAT AWAY FROM ME

    THE WAY YOUR SMILE JUST BEAMS
    THE WAY YOU SING OFF KEY
    THE WAY YOU HAUNT MY DREAMS
    NO THEY CAN'T TAKE THAT AWAY FROM ME

    WE MAY NEVER NEVER MEET AGAIN, ON THAT BUMPY
    ROAD TO LOVE
    BUT I'LL ALWAYS, ALWAYS KEEP THE MEMORY OF

    THE WAY YOU HOLD YOUR KNIFE
    THE WAY WE DANCED TILL THREE
    THE WAY YOU CHANGED MY LIFE
    NO THEY CAN'T TAKE THAT AWAY FROM ME

(While he sings softly, **CAROL** *keeps talking.)*

CAROL. And it was very sweet and stuff, but I don't understand any of it. I don't get how this happens to her. She...she has like this brand new life that has nothing to do with me, or dad, or my brothers or the 25 or so previous years of her life. How does this happen?. How does someone turn herself into someone completely different while I wasn't looking?. I can barely run my own life. Anyway, all this weirdness kept happening all throughout the visit. They...they even kissed in front of me. *(grimaces)* So, by the end of the visit, I was all set for them to go. At the airport, Mom went to the bathroom and I was in the airport alone with –

BOYFRIEND. It was nice to meet you.

*(***CAROL*** turns to talk to the ***BOYFRIEND*** for the first time.)*

CAROL. Yeah, it was good of you to come.

BOYFRIEND. You were weirded out by this.

CAROL. No, it was.

BOYFRIEND. You were.

CAROL. OK, yes. I so completely don't get what's going on. Who are you?

BOYFRIEND. Is it so hard to believe that. I could be interested in your mother?

CAROL. Well, yes. She was always like this terrifying authority mom figure. Now I gotta see her as a single gal with a dating life. This is just wrong.

(MOTHER *reenters, listens to the conversation.*)

BOYFRIEND. Your mom's a sweet woman. All she wants, all she ever wanted, is to have a happy daughter. That's it, you know? She just wants you to be happy with yourself.

CAROL. She never said that to me.

BOYFRIEND. No, she probably didn't. But she has said it to me, OK?

(CAROL *smiles.* MOTHER *enters. They give each other a hug.*)

CAROL. Oh, mom.

MOTHER. Good bye, sweetie. Do you need money? Here.

(MOTHER *hands* CAROL *some money.* MOTHER *and the* BOYFRIEND *leave with a wave.* CAROL *turns back to the audience.*)

CAROL. And so that was my week. I don't know. They got on the plane, back to California, and then onto Alaska for a two week cruise.

(CAROL *makes a brief gesture of* "What the hell?", *referring to the two week cruise. She shakes her head.* RITA *enters with an apron on.*)

CAROL. I don't know. I mean, is it just me? Is all of this so hard to swallow? Or should I look at this as a good sign in the larger scheme of things If she can do it, why can't I, right?

RITA. Lady, I just work here. Do you want another Diet Coke or what?

CAROL. Sure, make it a double. *(**RITA** starts to leave.)* Hey, Rita?

RITA. Yeah.

CAROL. Do you have karaoke tonight?

RITA. Karaoke's on Friday. Tonight we got bingo.

*(**RITA** slaps down a bingo card and exits. In the background, we hear the **BOYFRIEND** sing. **CAROL** joins him, looking wistfully at the bingo card.)*

CAROL & BOYFRIEND *(singing)*
THE WAY YOU WEAR YOUR HAT
THE WAY YOU SIP YOUR TEA
THE MEMORY OF ALL THAT
NO THEY CAN'T TAKE THAT AWAY FROM ME

THE END

HIT ME

By Patrick Cleary

CHARACTERS

Jimmy

Carl

HIT ME was performed on April 13, 2003, during the Boston Theater Marathon V at the Boston Playwright's Theatre. It was directed by Adam R. Perlman and produced by Speakeasy Stage Company. The cast was as follows:

JIMMY . . . . Tommy Day Carey
CARL . . . . Miguel Cervantes

(*SCENE: The living room of a lower middle class house.* **JIMMY** - *late 20s - paces. A few moments later, the door opens.* **CARL** - *early 30s - Jimmy's older brother, enters.*)

JIMMY. What took you so long?

(**CARL** *doesn't say a word. He approaches* **JIMMY**, *who takes a step back.* **CARL** *punches* **JIMMY** *in the gut, causing* **JIMMY** *to double over, winded. As Jimmy's head goes down,* **CARL** *knees him in the head, thrusting him backward.* **JIMMY**, *panting for breath, grabs the couch and uses it to hoist himself to his hands and knees.* **CARL** *calmly walks over and kicks* **JIMMY** *in the gut, sending him down to the floor again.*)

JIMMY. *(shakily sitting up)* Jesus Christ! Carl, wait –

(**CARL** *slaps* **JIMMY** *hard across the mouth.* **JIMMY** *covers his head with his arms and falls into the fetal position on the floor, whimpering.* **CARL** *sits down on the couch with* **JIMMY** *at his feet. After a moment, he grabs* **JIMMY** *by the hair and pulls him up so they are face-to-face.*)

CARL. What's the matter?

JIMMY. Hold on a minute. Just – *(He wipes blood from his nose.)* Just hold on.

(**CARL** *releases Jimmy's head and* **JIMMY** *rocks back and forth for a moment, holding onto his head and stomach.*)

CARL. Come on, little brother.

JIMMY. I know, I know –

CARL. This wasn't my idea, Jimmy –

JIMMY. Right. Right. Just hold on, I gotta –

CARL. Gotta what? There something more pressing on your schedule?

JIMMY. I just didn't realize…

CARL. Yeah?

JIMMY. It hurts.

CARL. No shit.

JIMMY. It hurts a lot.

CARL. That's kind of the point, isn't it?

JIMMY. I guess so. *(He touches his nose gingerly.)* Shit!

CARL. You want me to stop?

JIMMY. What?

CARL. Listen, you can't take it? I'll stop. I can leave right now, go back to work –

JIMMY. You can't –

CARL. Like I said, this wasn't my idea.

JIMMY. Carl, you can't –

CARL. They're gonna start missing me at work –

JIMMY. Okay –

CARL. I'm already in the doghouse there 'cause of my back –

JIMMY. Okay, okay!

> *(JIMMY pulls himself to his feet. He reaches for his face, as if to wipe away more blood, but stops. He drops his hands to his sides and squeezes his eyes shut.)*

JIMMY. Go ahead.

> *(CARL stands up, balls his hands into fists, and then unclenches them.)*

CARL. Shit.

JIMMY. *(opening his eyes)* What?

CARL. I don't know…

JIMMY. It's okay. Go ahead.

CARL. I lost my momentum.

JIMMY. Well, get it back!

CARL. It's not that easy –

JIMMY. Look, I'm sorry I messed you up –

CARL. I had to work myself up to this in the car –

JIMMY. It's my fault. I screwed up your rhythm.

CARL. I was doing good until you –

JIMMY. I know, I know. I said I'm sorry, didn't I?

CARL. Don't say you're sorry.

JIMMY. Okay.

CARL. Don't say anything at all.

JIMMY. Right.

CARL. It'll be easier if you just keep your mouth shut.

(JIMMY *starts to speak, then draws his finger across his lips, "zipping" them shut. He stands, waiting.* CARL *turns away, gathers his courage, and then runs at his brother. Just as he swings,* JIMMY *ducks, and* CARL *goes sailing past him, hitting only air.*)

CARL. Jesus Christ, Jimmy!

JIMMY. I didn't mean to do that.

CARL. Damnit!

JIMMY. It's really hard to just, you know, hold still!

CARL. Fuck this.

(CARL *turns away from* JIMMY *and walks towards the front door.*)

JIMMY. Where are you going?

CARL. Back to work.

(JIMMY *runs in front of* CARL *and blocks the front door.*)

JIMMY. You can't – I mean, you can't just go!

CARL. Watch me.

(CARL *reaches for the door, but* JIMMY *pushes him away.*)

JIMMY. C'mon, Carl.

CARL. I'm serious.

(JIMMY *pushes* CARL *backwards.*)

JIMMY. Yeah? So am I.

CARL. Get out of my fucking way.

(**CARL** *attempts to push past* **JIMMY**, *but* **JIMMY** *pushes him backwards again, hard.*)

JIMMY. Make me.

CARL. Stop it.

JIMMY. Like I said. Make me.

CARL. Don't make me –

JIMMY. What? WHAT? Don't make you WHAT?

(**CARL** *hunkers down and charges into* **JIMMY**, *attempting to ram him against the wall.* **JIMMY**, *however, is ready for this attack. He grabs* **CARL** *around the waist as the two connect and throws him to the floor.*)

CARL. Christ!

(**JIMMY** *goes to* **CARL** *and stands over him.*)

JIMMY. Get up, Carl.

CARL. *(remaining on the floor)* No.

JIMMY. Get UP, Carl.

CARL. No.

JIMMY. *(nudging* **CARL** *with his toe.)* Get the FUCK UP, Carl!

CARL. Jimmy –

JIMMY. Don't fuck with me, Carl. Not today. You promised.

CARL. I wasn't thinking –

JIMMY. Who asked you to THINK? I just need you to make good on your promise!

CARL. It's not gonna work, Jimmy.

(**JIMMY** *kicks* **CARL** *in the ribs.* **CARL** *gasps for breath and rolls over.*)

JIMMY. You promised!

CARL. Listen –

JIMMY. YOU PROMISED! YOU FUCKING PROMISED!

(**JIMMY** *kicks* **CARL**, *over and over.* **CARL** *grabs his stomach and crawls away on his knees and his free hand. He hides behind the couch.* **JIMMY** *starts after* **CARL**, *but* **CARL** *holds up two hands, in surrender.*)

CARL. LISTEN! JIMMY!

(JIMMY stands rigid, his hands clenching and unclenching, his body shaking. Finally, he deflates, and sits down on the couch.)

JIMMY. *(a plea)* You promised, Carl. You promised you'd do this.

(CARL slowly raises up, keeping JIMMY within his line-of-sight at all times.)

CARL. Jimmy, listen to me.

JIMMY. Nobody does what I ask them to.

CARL. You're not listening. I need you to pay attention.

JIMMY. Why is it always so hard? *(looks at CARL)* Why can't you just do what I ask you to? Why can't anybody just do what I ask? SHE wouldn't do ANYTHING I asked her to do. Not ONE FUCKING THING –

CARL. Look at me, Jimmy. Hey! *(JIMMY looks at him.)* We're not concentrating on her right now, am I right?

JIMMY. I'm just saying –

CARL. I'm just saying. We're not talking about her. Right? *(pause)* Right?

JIMMY. Yeah, okay.

CARL. I'm gonna help you, but – *(JIMMY starts to protest.)* BUT... I don't think this is gonna work.

JIMMY. Like you know –

CARL. Telephone records.

JIMMY. What?

CARL. You called me from this house when all this was supposedly going on. How you gonna account for that?

JIMMY. I – Jesus, Carl, I don't know!

CARL. See? You weren't thinking.

JIMMY. So you think I'm stupid. Is that it? You think I'm a fucking retard or something –

CARL. Jimmy! Jimmy, listen to me. I didn't think of it either, 'til just now.

JIMMY. Christ, Carl. *(He stands up, begins to pace. CARL moves out from behind the couch.)* I didn't think about that at all –

CARL. Well, now we have.

JIMMY. You know what? I am a fucking retard.

CARL. Calm down.

JIMMY. No. No, Carl. I'm a goddamn moron. Why don't you go? Just go. I shouldn't have gotten you involved.

CARL. What are you gonna do?

JIMMY. I don't know. Oh, fuck, who am I kidding? I'm gonna call the cops –

CARL. No.

JIMMY. What else am I gonna do?

CARL. We'll think of something.

JIMMY. Yeah, right. That turned out so well, right?

CARL. I said we'll think of something.

JIMMY. No. I was stupid to get you involved in the first place –

CARL. Well, I am now. We're gonna work on this together. We'll get you out of this together.

JIMMY. I'm sorry about kicking you.

CARL. Don't worry about that.

JIMMY. I lost it there. I just…I just lost it.

CARL. I know.

JIMMY. I've been losing my temper a lot, lately.

CARL. Yeah.

JIMMY. No shit, right? *(He smiles at* **CARL,** *but seeing the look on his brother's face, quickly suppresses it.)* Right.

CARL. Jimmy, I gotta ask you something.

JIMMY. Yeah?

CARL. Did you mean to…Never mind.

JIMMY. You sure?

CARL. I don't wanna know.

JIMMY. Okay.

CARL. So we'd better think of something. Where is she?

JIMMY. In the bedroom.

CARL. Okay. You get cleaned up, I'm gonna go scope the damage.

JIMMY. Carl?

CARL. Yeah?

JIMMY. It's bad. It's really bad.

CARL. I figured that.

(**CARL** *heads toward the stairs while* **JIMMY** *walks towards the bathroom.*)

JIMMY. Carl?

CARL. Yeah?

JIMMY. *(Pause)* I – Nothing. Never mind.

(**JIMMY** *exits to the bathroom.* **CARL** *looks up the stairs, pauses, then begins to climb.*)

(*Lights down.*)

SKATEBOARDS

By Norman Lasca

CHARACTERS

Rose

Jason

Stanley

SKATEBOARDS was produced by the Nora Theatre Company and was directed by Ronn Smith. The cast was as follows:

ROSE . . . . Bobbie Steinbach
STANLEY . . . . James Bodge
JASON . . . . Adam Howe

*(At lights, **STANLEY** and **ROSE**, a couple in their 80s, sit on a park bench. **STANLEY** watches skateboards pass back and forth, **ROSE** knits.)*

STANLEY. *(bitter)* Look at 'em.

ROSE. Here we go again.

STANLEY. *Skateboards...*

ROSE. Two days now, Stanley, and you haven't changed the topic.

STANLEY. Boards with wheels on 'em...

ROSE. You can't even *see* them with your eyesight.

STANLEY. Planks of wood that *roll* across the ground...

ROSE. *Blurry* planks of wood as far as you're concerned.

STANLEY. I am profoundly disappointed, Rose.

ROSE. We know you are, Stanley.

STANLEY. Is this the 21st century?

ROSE. It's not 1945, that's for sure.

STANLEY. I thought people would be *flying* by now!

ROSE. Always the dreamer.

STANLEY. I thought we'd be floating down the streets on anti-gravity machines! Breathing underwater! Colonizing Mars! I thought they'd have cures for cancer, heart disease, diabetes...

ROSE. *(to herself)* But no...

STANLEY. But no!

ROSE. *(to self)* Instead, here we are...

STANLEY. Instead, we get a buncha kids showin' up and takin' over the park with skateboards!

ROSE. It could be worse, Stanley. They could have guns.

STANLEY. Whizzing up and down, monopolizing the public restroom, and generally making it a hazard for the tax-paying members of the community!...

ROSE. Don't forget the way they're dressed.

STANLEY. Dressing like a bunch of circus freaks!

ROSE. *(to self)* Now, isn't that a…

STANLEY. *(overlaps, fast)* Now, isn't *that* a son of a bitch!

> *(Brief pause. **ROSE** nods to herself. She holds her hand out to **STANLEY**. After a beat, he grudgingly reaches into his pocket and produces a nickel. He hands it to her.)*

ROSE. Thank you.

> *(**ROSE** drops the nickel into her bra. After a brief pause, **STANLEY** turns to **ROSE**; then, deliberately.)*

STANLEY. I mean it, Rose. It's a son of a *bitch.*

> *(The two look at one another for a moment before **STAN-LEY** reaches into his pocket and gives **ROSE** another nickel. **ROSE** takes the nickel and silently puts it into her bra. She faces the audience again. Pause)*

STANLEY Don't know what you think you're gonna get with those. Charging me a nickel every time I curse.

ROSE. I'm going to buy myself an ice cream cone.

STANLEY. Be a while before you get an ice cream cone that way.

> *(**STANLEY** turns to face the audience again. Pause)*

ROSE. We used to roller-skate, Stanley.

STANLEY. Mmm. Didn't we.

ROSE. We did. We used to roller-skate every Thursday night. At the rink out in Waltham.

STANLEY. *(sarcastic)* Weren't those the days.

ROSE. While Millie and George stayed home with the sitter…

STANLEY. Twisted my ankle I don't know how many times.

ROSE. You were Fred Astaire on roller-skates. The most elegant skater there was.

STANLEY. Mmm. And now I've got the knees to prove it.

ROSE. *(dreaming)* While Oscar Peterson played Broadway…

STANLEY. While Joe McCarthy ran the Inquisition.

ROSE. While Bing Crosby sang songs for us...

STANLEY. While we went and entered a land war in Southeast Asia.

ROSE. While George met Lily, and Millie met Roger...

STANLEY. While George turned down Dartmouth for a football scholarship at Worcester Polytech, while Millie went through divorce number one.

ROSE. You were the best skater there was, Stanley...

STANLEY. Worcester Polytech, Rose...

ROSE. You were the best skater there was...

STANLEY. Hmmph. *(pauses)* Buncha bullshit.

> (**ROSE** *does nothing. Pause*)

I said, "Bunch of bullshit."

> (**ROSE** *says nothing, does nothing, wants nothing.* **STANLEY** *watches her, sees this, and then decides to give her some change anyway. Just as he's digging in his pocket a skateboard rolls onto the stage and stops at* **STANLEY**'*S feet. Long pause as* **STANLEY** *stares at the skateboard as though it were an alien.*)

STANLEY *(cont'd)* What's this?

ROSE. Looks like a skateboard.

STANLEY. What is it doing here?

ROSE. Must belong to one of the kids.

> (*Pause.* **STANLEY** *rises and walks centerstage. He should walk very slowly, like an "old man." When he gets center stage, he peers out into the audience, squinting. Pause*)

STANLEY. *(to the audience)* Hey!...Hey, one of your pieces of kindling just rolled away from you!...

> (*no response*)

STANLEY. I say you lost one of your rolly logs!...

> (*no response. To* **ROSE:**)

Must be *deaf* circus freaks.

> (*After a pause,* **STANLEY** *starts back to the bench. He stops suddenly, his attention caught by the skateboard.*)

STANLEY Did you see that?

ROSE. See what?

STANLEY. It *moved.*

ROSE. What moved?

STANLEY. The *skateboard.* It rolled backward.

ROSE. Things don't just roll backward, Stanley.

STANLEY. My whole skeletal structure's been rolling backward for twenty years now.

ROSE. That's different.

STANLEY. *(firm)* It moved.

(pause)

Suppose I'd better get it out of the way before somebody trips over it.

ROSE. There's no one here *to* trip over it.

STANLEY. Someone could come along, I mean.

ROSE. A pigeon, maybe.

STANLEY. I feel a civic responsibility here, Rose.

ROSE. Have it your way, Stanley. Only make sure it's not you who's doing the tripping.

*(After a pause, **STANLEY** approaches the skateboard. He looks at it. Slowly, he bends down to pick it up. He stops, his attention caught by something. He squints at the skateboard. Pause.)*

ROSE. What is it?

STANLEY. Says here that skateboarding isn't a crime.

ROSE. I don't suppose it is. Balancing on a board and pushing yourself across the ground.

STANLEY. That all there is to it? "Balancing on a board and pushing yourself across the ground"?

ROSE. You know as well as I do, Stanley. You've seen 'em.

*(**STANLEY** nods. After a long pause, he very slowly places a foot on the board, just so that the tip of his foot is touching it. Equally slowly, he rolls the board back and forth a tiny bit. He takes his foot off the board. Pause.)*

ROSE. What are you doing?

STANLEY. Seein' what kind of improvement this thing is on roller-skates.

ROSE. *(cautious)* Well?

STANLEY. Smooth.

ROSE. There you have it.

> *(Pause. Very slowly,* STANLEY *places his foot fully on the board. He rolls the board back and forth again.)*

ROSE. Stanley... ?

STANLEY. Can't imagine what kind of bearings they've got in these wheels...

ROSE. I'm going to count to three, Stanley, and if you're not off that board by the time I'm finished I don't know what. One...Two...

> (STANLEY *raises his other foot onto the board.)*

Stanley!...Oh!

> (STANLEY *successfully stands on the skateboard, teetering at first, but then gradually gaining control until he stands comfortably.* STANLEY *looks around the audience, around the park, off in direction from which the board did not come.)*

ROSE.*(stern, enunciating)* Two and a half, Stanley.

STANLEY. Amazing. I can see the fountain from here. Just a – just a coupla extra inches, but – I can see the fountain clear as day...

ROSE. Two and three *quarters!*...

STANLEY. See the pigeons...

ROSE. Two and three and a *half* quarters, Stanley!...

STANLEY. The Abe Lincoln statue, the pretzel stand...

ROSE. Two and three *quarters* quarters!...

STANLEY. S'a good thing I'm not facing the restrooms, Rose. Don't know if I could handle seeing circus freaks with this level of clarity.

ROSE. Three, Stanley! *Three!*

STANLEY. Give me a push, Rose. I don't think I can balance and push myself at the same time.

ROSE. Have you lost your mind?!

STANLEY. Why, you hear wind whistling through my ears?

ROSE. You get down off that thing this instant!

STANLEY. Well, I guess I'll just have to try doing it myself, then.

*(**STANLEY** makes a big show of trying to push and balance.)*

Ahhhhhhhhhh... Unnnnnnnnhhhh...

ROSE. No, no! All right, all right! I'll give you a push!

*(**STANLEY** stops, waits. Slowly, achingly slowly, **ROSE** rises from the bench and makes her way over to **STANLEY**.)*

STANLEY. On my back. Put your hands on my back.

*(**ROSE** tentatively puts her hands on **STANLEY**'s back.)*

Around my chest. Put 'em around my chest. For support.

*(Very slowly, **ROSE** moves her arms around so that she is holding **STANLEY** from behind, hugging him almost. Her face pressed into his back. **STANLEY** puts his arms out like wings – for balance.)*

STANLEY. Now... push.

*(Very slowly, **ROSE** begins to inch **STANLEY** forward, **ROSE** pushed up against **STANLEY**, **STANLEY** with his arms outspread. They move forward incredibly slowly.)*

STANLEY. Birds, Rose!...I can see birds!...Grey...white... black...feeding on crusts of bread...Feathers incandescent in the sunlight...*(amazed)* Clear as day, no blurriness...

*(The sound of music fades in, a gentle breeze. As **STANLEY** continues, **JASON**, a kid of about eighteen, wearing torn-up shirt, jeans, dyed hair, piercings enters from the opposite side of the stage and stops, clearly shocked by what he sees.)*

STANLEY. And…and there's Mr. Weinstein's market…and the Laundromat…The – the little bodega across from the café…It's incredible, Rose. You've got to try it. No, no. Stop. Let me off. I'll push you.

(Very slowly, ROSE *stops.* STANLEY *is in the process of dismounting when he sees* JASON. *From* STANLEY*'s look,* ROSE *turns and sees* JASON, *too. The music comes to an abrupt halt.)*

JASON. Um. Can I have my board back?

*(*STANLEY *and* ROSE *say nothing.* JASON *comes up, takes his board, and skates off leaving* STANLEY *and* ROSE *staring after him. Long pause.* STANLEY *slowly makes his way to the bench, followed by* ROSE. *They sit and look out into the audience as they were at the top of the play. Long pause.)*

STANLEY. Must've rolled away from him while he was in the bathroom.

ROSE. I suppose so.

(long pause)

STANLEY. Buy you an ice cream?

ROSE. Chocolate.

*(*STANLEY *nods. Blackout.)*

YOUR BETTER BUTCH FASHION

By Margaret Broucek

CHARACTERS

Linda

*(**SCENE**: Rabbi's office. There is a desk with many books and a candy jar on it and a desk chair behind it, as well as two chairs in front of the desk, facing it. There is also a couch in the middle of the stage, with a coffee table in front of it. On the coffee table are more books and a menorah. **LINDA SHIFFSTEIN**, a woman around 50, enters the office with her husband. The rabbi and the husband are imagined by the audience and are not portrayed by actors. **LINDA** carries her purse with her everywhere on stage.)*

LINDA. Thank you for seeing us, Rabbi. We don't know each other so well because Bert and I sit in the back at temple – and sometimes don't even sit because of Bert's condition. Oh, no, please! There's nothing wrong with him! Except sometimes he has trouble breathing when he's thinking about it.

(She indicates one of the chairs for visitors.)

Can you sit, now, Bert? So sit.

(She doesn't sit, but comes downstage, facing the audience.)

So, Rabbi, something you should know…is…our daughter…is a butch. I'm not saying *butcher*, that's a job. We should be so lucky to have a butcher in the family. I'm saying butch, which is a term that a complete stranger called my Marilyn on our Columbus Avenue, in front of her mother.

It was enough we knew she was a lesbian, now she has to be a butch – which my sister Joan says is the one playing the male role in a homosexual relationship. "*Bubbeleh,*" that's what a person should call you as they walk past on the street. Why should someone say aloud a statement like "Look at that butch"? So she doesn't go in for skirts, is that criminal? Her sister, Irene, is *not* a butch. Thank God. I would not wish two butch daughters on a cat!

(She sits in the other chair.)

I have asked all of the analysts in the family, "What is it that happened? Was I too pushy? Was it too much I encourage them to be who they should want?" I have turned my daughter into something our people have not seen since that woman who wrote, "A rose is a rose is a rose is a whatever the hell it is!"

Bert, you should know, blames himself. He wanted a boy. He called her "Champ" when she was in the womb. Big deal! But babies hear in the womb, according to Bert and the New York Times. Here's a news-alert for you, Bert – babies hear indigestion. They hear when you pass gas. That's what babies hear.

Sorry, Rabbi.

So, we have said to our girls if you are going to be something, do it well, be the best. This is all we ask. And I do not think a dirty suit jacket from the Jewish League thrift and boots a motorcycle person wears is striving for some sort of butch perfection. This is just meshuga to me. I said, "Marilyn, we can do better for butch." We went to Saks. You think I'm kidding? We went to Saks.

(She gets up and moves to stand behind the couch.)

Tommy Hilfiger has a jacket and pants that are masculine yet have a style, make a statement for a person walking down Columbus Avenue. If you're going to walk with your mother and be a butch, wear Tommy Hilfiger is all I'm saying. Again, with shoes, let's get good shoes. Kenneth Cole ankle boots with the squared toe, which I have seen in the catalog on men I would leave Bert for. Let's wear those shoes!

(She moves around to sit on the couch and rearranges the books on the coffee table.)

Then, Marilyn wears a chain from a belt loop to her wallet in the back pocket. I don't know from chains, but this looks like something I did not raise a child to wear. Marilyn says it's wallet protection, and Rabbi, it's true that there are people in this city who will take your wallet, and to those people I say, "Marilyn has maybe a dollar in a wallet." She's a butch, not a butcher, after all. She has no job. But she has chained her wallet to her pants.

(She pulls tissues out of her purse and begins to wipe the coffee table.)

Och, so much to change.

Another thing I told her, when a person directs people to, "Look at that butch," the correct response does not involve raising a particular finger. God sees fingers. Am I right? God makes a note on fingers.

(She pulls out each candle from the menorah and wipes it off.)

So, clothing we can change. Who she should meet and date is a more difficult aspect. Bert and I think that meeting a nice Jewish girl is not so easy in a place called the "Clit Club," and I am not using that term of my own volition. This is the name of a club that gives away books of matches for people to leave in their mothers' houses. How would you like to be cleaning your own living room and have to read such a word? When we were young, you met at the Waldorf. Now you meet at a club with the name of a thing we women didn't even know we had until well into our twenties. Every time she goes to that club, I pray to God they are out of matches. I hope, also, that someone else's Jewish daughter is there in Donna Karan. She's just changed after coming off her rounds at Mt. Sinai. They meet. They fall in love. Please God. We're done.

(She gets up and makes her way back to the Rabbi's desk.)

She would prefer to meet someone with a pierced face. My hand to God. I suppose this is so the woman can chain her face to her pants.

(She sits in a chair at the desk.)

So, why are we here when it seems that I have everything working in harmony? Because, Rabbi, Marilyn did not come home from that club last week. No call. No consideration for our worries at an age when a stroke is not impossible. Bert's sister, Adele, had a stroke when her son missed her birthday. Now she can't smell an orange. How would you like to live a life in which of all your fruits smell like masking tape? So the very next night, Bert and I went to the Clit Club. It's not so hard to find when you have the matches with the address. Bert was forty minutes in the bedroom getting ready. Usually he's not so concerned about his attire. All of a sudden, he's worried about his shoes matching his pants.

Thinking in advance, I asked Bert to bring his X-ray. He owns an X-ray film from last year that shows a dark spot on his lungs. The doctors said it's nothing, but I'm thinking it could come in handy with figuring out who in the bar is a doctor and who is not.

(She takes a candy out of the jar.)

About how old is the candy, Rabbi?

(beat)

Is that a fact?

(She puts the candy back into the jar.)

I had called the car service and the man was waiting at the curb when we got down. He asked where we wanted to go. I just gave the address. There is no need to say "clit" to a car service driver. This address is in a part of town where I would not want to drop off a cat! Bert tells the driver that we are going to a ladies club, which I think makes it sound like I'm a stripper or I enjoy a stripper. Thank you, Marilyn.

(She gets up to act out the scene.)

When the driver has found the club, Bert and I head right to the door. There is a woman standing outside the door of the club. I say "woman," but who knows. She tells us that this is a woman's bar, to which I say that we are meeting our daughter and I show her the matches.

This club is not doing such great business from what we can see inside. There are maybe three women in the place. So to help out, Bert ordered a round for the house. The bartender said that this charge comes to a total of fifty-seven dollars. This is the same price our co-op was in 1976!

One of the patrons thanks Bert for her blue drink, and he feels compelled to tell her that he is a married man.

Marilyn was not among the hundred and fifty women who had come into the bar by 1:30. I know. I was stationed by the door. Bert was at the bar holding up his X-ray. No one even knew it was a lung!

There were three women on a stage in Victorian underclothes. There was no point to this show. They did not sing. They did not dance. They just stood around with their hands on their hips. I hope they have no dreams of being Rockettes. If this is club life today, I thank God I am old. We had clubs with people who could sing. We had people who could tell a joke that would make your appendix burst. Now they have women who know how to put on their underwear.

At 2:45 in the morning, we gave up. When we walked out, Bert started across the street and was nearly smacked by a truck.

(She moves back to the couch and reclines a bit from exhaustion)

The next morning, I found Marilyn asleep in her room – her room which I painted peach to bring sunniness into her life. She did the rest. It looks now like the peach room of death. She tells me, in her stupor, that she's moving out of this room and into some place that I don't know what color it is, but I'm guessing it's a dark, dark place. Our Marilyn is moving in with a woman she met at that club. You know what the draw was? The shoes. This woman has invited Marilyn and her shoes to move in. She probably thinks since Marilyn has the wallet protection, she can afford rent. This moving-in will happen when the woman gets back from Europe. Would you like to know who she's in Europe with, Rabbi? Her current girlfriend. According to Marilyn, she's going to break up with the girl on the trip. That's nice, eh? That's a quality person. May I show you a picture of this woman? Yes, we're lucky; we have a picture.

(She gets a picture out of her purse and takes it over to the Rabbi. It is a photo of a multi-pierced face.)

So something you should know is my daughter is going to live with a woman who is a walking rack of earrings.

(She sits in the chair next to her husband and leans toward the Rabbi.)

So here's the thing, Rabbi. Bert and I have noticed that some of our women rabbis are not so interested in men. Can you deny this! So let's suppose Marilyn comes to service and stays after to ask a few religious questions. This is not so hard. I can make a nice brunch with lox and we have a woman rabbi over to the house. What do you say, eh? We'd like you for this Saturday, Rabbi Judith. OK? Here's the address.

(She slaps a piece of paper from her purse onto the desk.)

END

DATE NIGHT

By Glen Doyle

CHARACTERS

Hostess

Brenda

Harold

Jennifer

Margaret

TIME

The present

PLACE

Function room of hotel

*(Several women are onstage, mingling, glass of wine in hand making polite conversation in excited anticipation. **HAROLD** is sitting at a round table, partially obscured by all the women on stage.)*

HOSTESS. Thank you, ladies. May I have your attention. Good evening ladies and gentlemen, and welcome to this month's 5 minute Speed Dating for middle-aged, divorced, separated and otherwise available dysfunctional singles. Ladies, you all know the rules – five minutes to get to know the man of your dreams. And gentlemen, you know the rules too – *no touching*. At the sound of the bell, ladies, go to the table of your choice and begin your 5 minute Speed Date. Good luck ladies. *(rings bell)*

*(The women criss-cross the stage and exit. Initially no-one stops at **HAROLD**'s table. After a few seconds **BRENDA** sits at **HAROLD**'s table. She is bubbly, energetic and alive – **HAROLD** is timid)*

BRENDA. Hello, I'm Brenda.

HAROLD. Pleased to meet you. I'm Harold.

BRENDA. Harold? That's a nice name.

HAROLD. Thank you.

BRENDA. I always believe that a name tells a lot about someone, don't you?

HAROLD. Yes, I suppose it does

BRENDA. I mean, Harold. That's a name with character. It's strong, bold, it conjures up visions of a man of action power and strength. What do you do, for a job I mean?

HAROLD. Me? Well, I'm unemployed at the moment.

BRENDA. Oh. ...Oh...Well, what do you...normally do... when you are...employed?

HAROLD. I'm an electrician.

BRENDA. Electrician…Oh…An unemployed electrician.

HAROLD. Well, that's one way of putting it.

BRENDA. That's the only way of putting it. Isn't it?

HAROLD. I suppose.

BRENDA. Well, anyway. I'm kind of looking for someone who is at least gainfully employed, you know, with a pulse and a paycheck, single, unattached, reasonably good looking, and can maintain an interesting and intelligent conversation.

HAROLD. And you're looking for all that in one man?

BRENDA. Hopefully, yes. All women are, aren't they?

HAROLD. Are they?

BRENDA. Yes, of course. We want the whole package. We want it all. We want security, romance, honesty, loyalty, intelligence, and love.

HAROLD. Well, one out of six isn't bad is it?

BRENDA. Which one do you have…don't tell me…you'll only get my hopes up. So what's a guy like you doing at a place like this?

HAROLD. Well, I just…

BRENDA. Have you been here before?

HAROLD. Well, I was….

BRENDA. This is my first time. Thought I'd just give it a try. Not going too well so far is it?

HAROLD. I'm the first one you've spoken to.

BRENDA. That's what I mean.

HAROLD. You're certainly quick to judge aren't you? You're certainly one to jump to a quick conclusion.

BRENDA. In case you haven't noticed – It's called speed dating! I have five minutes to check you out, study you, size you up and then write down your number – if I'm interested – or toss you aside like yesterday's leftovers!

HAROLD. Well, that's romantic isn't it?

BRENDA. It's *five minute* speed dating!

HAROLD. Yes. but, I haven't had much time to talk about myself have I? I haven't been given the opportunity to express my hopes, my dreams, my aspirations, my innermost soulful thoughts about life, relationships, the universe.

BRENDA. Is that a English accent you have?...That's sooo interesting. I knew someone from England once – Brian Miller – did you know him?

HAROLD. No. No, I can't say I did

BRENDA. He was unemployed too – no ambition – no spark – no drive whatsover...you very much remind me of him

HAROLD. I do?

BRENDA. Yes. So...are you...widowed, divorced?

HAROLD. I'm recently separated.

BRENDA. Oh...Oh...Wrong answer. This is not gonna be my night.

HAROLD. That's not very nice is it?

BRENDA. True though – I steer clear of men recently separated, recently divorced, recently widowed and recently married.

HAROLD. That can't leave you with many to choose from, can it?

BRENDA. There has to be someone out there for me doesn't there? That's why I'm here. To find the man of my dreams –and look at me – I end up with an unemployed nightmare!

(lights flash – bell rings)

Oops...there's the signal, gotta go – good luck – Harold!?

HOSTESS. Time to move to another table, ladies – and make your choice of the man of your dreams

*(Ladies criss-cross the stage, and exit as **JENNIFER** sits at Harold's table. She's attractive, sexy and flirty – he's feeling a little bolder.)*

JENNIFER. Hello, my name's Jennifer.

HAROLD. Jennifer, that's a nice name.

JENNIFER. Thank you.

HAROLD. *(hesitant at first)* I always believe that a name tells a lot about someone, don't you?

JENNIFER. Yes, I suppose it does. What's your name?

HAROLD. Harold. Harold Spencer – the third!

JENNIFER. Oooh. That's certainly a name with character.

HAROLD. Character, yes.

JENNIFER. It's strong, it's bold.

HAROLD. Strong, bold, yes.

JENNIFER. It conjures up visions of a man of sophistication, style and elegance. What do you do, for a job I mean?

HAROLD. Me? I'm in the field of…electronic fusion. Currently working with …electrical particles for the domestic and…international markets.

JENNIFER. How impressive. There's a big demand for that is there?

HAROLD. Oh yes. I keep busy. I'm putting in 60 hour weeks. Busy, busy, busy.

JENNIFER. Well, that's nice. My ex-husband was just like you.

HAROLD. Really?

JENNIFER. A crazy workaholic.

HAROLD. Oh Really?

JENNIFER. Yes. Worked all hours. It completely ruined our marriage.

HAROLD. Well, I don't always work that hard, sometimes it's just 40 hours a week. It just depends on the demand for electrical supply.

JENNIFER. Oh, this won't do. You see I'm looking for someone who's a little more laid back – someone who's ready to take it easy and can just put their feet up.

HAROLD. I can put my feet up.

JENNIFER. I'm at that stage where I want to enjoy life, slow down and just smell the coffee.

HAROLD. I can smell coffee. I like coffee.

JENNIFER. What a man does for a living doesn't bother me. He could a plumber, a carpenter, an electrician.

HAROLD. Hold on, I am a...

JENNIFER. You know what I find really attractive in a man?

HAROLD. Yes I think I do

JENNIFER. You do?

HAROLD. Yes. You like someone who is gainfully employed, you know, with a pulse and a paycheck, single, unattached, reasonably good looking, and can maintain an interesting and intelligent conversation. And you want the whole package. You want it all. You want security, romance, honesty, loyalty, intelligence, and love.

JENNIFER. Where did you get all that from?

HAROLD. That's what all women want isn't it?

JENNIFER. Not this woman. I want the bohemian type. Someone who is artistic, creative, someone who bucks the system and lives outside the box.

HAROLD. I can live outside the box. I used to live *in* a box

JENNIFER. No. You're just like my ex. A lot of women want that. Not me. I just want a lover. Someone to make love to me every single day. Someone I can just hold close and take into my bosom.

HAROLD. I can do bosoms.

JENNIFER. No. You're a hard worker...too ambitious for me.

HAROLD. But...I was thinking...you...me...we could...

(lights flash – bell rings)

JENNIFER. Oooh. There's the signal. Nice meeting you... Harold was it?

HOSTESS. Yes, ladies. It's time to make another selection for the man of your dreams on Date Night.

*(Ladies criss-cross the stage, and exit as **MARGARET** – sophisticated lawyer type – sits at **HAROLD**'s table – **HAROLD** is now a little confused)*

MARGARET. Oh. Hello – you're leaving?

HAROLD. I'm sorry.

MARGARET. I say one word and you're leaving just like that?

HAROLD. I'm sorry I have to –

MARGARET. My goodness. I usually make a better first impression than this

HAROLD. I'm sorry. This just isn't for me.

MARGARET. What's not for you? This – this ...is not for you?

HAROLD. No. I didn't mean that. No. It's not you. It's the whole thing. This speed dating thing just doesn't work for me I'm afraid

MARGARET. It doesn't work for anyone, does it?

HAROLD. It doesn't?

MARGARET. If it did, they wouldn't keep having them every month, would they?

HAROLD. I suppose not. So why do you come to them?

MARGARET. I'm the eternal optimist my dear. I still believe there's an honest, loving caring, tender soul-mate waiting for me just around the corner.

HAROLD. *(looks around the corner)* And you think he might be here?

MARGARET. I didn't actually say "he," did I?

HAROLD. Oooh. You're a ...lesbian then?

MARGARET. No. Just kidding, silly. Though based on what I see tonight, the lesbian option just might be worth considering.

HAROLD. Do they have speed dating for lesbians?

MARGARET. They have everything for lesbians

HAROLD. They do?

MARGARET. I wouldn't know would I? I've never been with another woman...except in a threesome of course.

HAROLD. Threesome? You've done a threesome?

MARGARET. Hasn't everyone?

HAROLD. You've had a threesome?

MARGARET. No. Silly. I have enough trouble getting a two-some to work than to worry about a threesome.

HAROLD. It's no worry.

MARGARET. So what brings you here? In search of your dream woman on date night?

HAROLD. It seemed like a good idea at the time.

MARGARET. So how is it going so far?

HAROLD. Oh I don't know. How much can you really know about a person in just five minutes? Some people don't know each other after five years, do they?

MARGARET. Well, I already know a lot about you.

HAROLD. You do?

MARGARET. Oh yes. I know that you are intelligent; sensitive; creative; dedicated; humble; and a very generous soul.

HAROLD. You can tell all that about me?

MARGARET. Of course not silly – just kidding.

HAROLD. Kidding? The humble part – and the generous bit?

MARGARET. All of it.

HAROLD. All of it?

MARGARET. Well, maybe not all of it.

HAROLD. Which parts were you not kidding about – intelligent?

MARGARET. Kidding.

HAROLD. Sensitive?

MARGARET. Kidding.

HAROLD. Creative.

MARGARET. Kidding – I'm just kidding. You could be all those things.

HAROLD. I could be all those things.

MARGARET. You probably are all those things.

HAROLD. I am all those things.

MARGARET. Humble?

HAROLD. Well, maybe not humble, no…You're probably all those things. You're intelligent; witty; charming; sensitive; inspiring; challenging; sophisticated.

MARGARET. Mm…mm…go on…go on.

HAROLD. And you're probably a damn good kisser.

MARGARET. I beg your pardon?

HAROLD. I said, you're probably a damn good listener.

MARGARET. The answer is yes – to both.

HAROLD. So have you met any good prospects tonight?

MARGARET. Slim pickings I'm afraid. But then again, where am I going to find a rich and handsome knight in shining armor to whisk me off my feet and ride off into the sunset? Certainly not here.

HAROLD. Certainly not here.

MARGARET. And you? What are you looking for?

HAROLD. Well, it would have to be a female.

MARGARET. That's good to know.

HAROLD. I've always been crazy about women.

MARGARET. Crazy?

HAROLD. Well, they drive me crazy actually.

MARGARET. And you still come back for more?

HAROLD. Yes.

MARGARET. Like lemmings to the sea.

HAROLD. Yes.

MARGARET. Like cattle eating the cactus.

HAROLD. Yes.

MARGARET. Like praying mantis –

HAROLD. I think you've made the point.

MARGARET. I think I did, didn't I?

HAROLD. You know…I was wondering…would you…be interested…perhaps…in having a drink later?

MARGARET. With you?

HAROLD. …Yes.

MARGARET. This is speed dating….you don't actually go on a date with anyone, silly.

HAROLD. You don't?

MARGARET. It's speed dating.

(lights flash – bell rings)

MARGARET. Bye…See you next month!!!

HOSTESS. Now it's time ladies to select the man of your choice, the man of your dreams, your date night man of the month.

*(Ladies criss cross the stage – **HAROLD** looks expectantly around – the ladies all exit – leaving **HAROLD** staring blankly into the audience.)*

FLUSHED

By Joshua Scher

CHARACTERS

DOVE – an unfortunate young professional (late twenties to early thirties).

BEATRICE – a Polish immigrant who works for a night cleaning service (twenties).

TIME

Late last night.

PLACE

The modern men's bathroom in Peter Luger's Steak House.

Flushed was directed by Ilana Brownstein for Next Stages. The cast was as follows:

DOVE . . . . Nathaniel McIntyre
BEATRICE . . . . Stacy Fischer

*(SCENE: A modern men's bathroom – from out of a toilet stall door, sprawls the bottom half of a man, **DOVE**, face down.)*

*(A cleaning woman, **BEATRICE**, enters with mop and pail and wearing headphones. She places items and exits. She returns carrying cleaning products. She places them in a sink. She exits and returns with rolls of toilet paper and stocks the first stall. The toilet in the first stall flushes as she exits to the second stall (the one with the body), when a light overhead flickers. Noticing, she exits, carrying the remaining rolls with her. She re-enters quickly, carrying a light bulb and a step stool. She burns herself, changing the bulb and lets out a small Polish curse. The legs stir slightly.)*

(She tends her burn in the sink and finally begins to mop. With wide strokes and leading with her rear, she advances across the room backwards towards the legs. She sings the lyrics to Sisco's Thong Song*or a similar such song.)*

DOVE. Hello?

(slightly louder)

Hello-o?

(She breaks into the bridge of the song.)

DOVE. Goddamnit!

(yelling)

HELLO!

(She's grooving, singing the chorus of the song now, until she backs into his legs and freezes.)

DOVE. Thank Christ.

---

* See Music Use Note page 3

(She turns, looks down, screams, and flees the bathroom. Beat)

DOVE. Shit.

(beat)

Hello? Please. I won't – I need help. I've, ah, fallen, and I...Oh for fuck's sake.

(The door slowly opens. BEATRICE darts her head in and out.)

BEATRICE. The restaurant's closed.

DOVE. You're back! You're back, oh you're a wonderful human being.

BEATRICE. The restaurant is closed.

DOVE. Yeah I know I –

BEATRICE. You shouldn't be here.

DOVE. Well, I agree. And I –

BEATRICE. I am calling police.

DOVE. *(raising his voice)* No, don't –

(lowering his voice)

Don't call the police. There's no need for the police. I'm not here to – I'm a customer.

BEATRICE. The restaurant is closed.

DOVE. Yes, I know. We've been over this. I know the restaurant is closed. I'm not supposed to be here. I don't want to be here. I want to leave. I am trying to leave. I would very much like to leave, it's just that I...am... stuck.

BEATRICE. *(now inside door)* Drunk?

DOVE. What?

BEATRICE. You are drunk?

DOVE. No. I am not drunk. I'm stuck. I was drunk, but now I'm stuck.

BEATRICE. Why haven't you gotten out?

DOVE. BECAUSE I'M STUCK!

(She flinches back and the door shuts.)

DOVE. Hello? HELLO?

(sighs)

Shit. Sorry. I'm sorry. I didn't mean to yell, I...I am very uncomfortable. Hello? I was at the restaurant very late. I got stuck, I must have passed out and no one saw me. Hello. Please. I didn't mean to scare you. I'm sorry. Now could you please come help me. I really could use some help. Please.

BEATRICE. *(opening door)* You shouldn't yell.

DOVE. Oh thank God.

(beat)

Sorry. You're right. I, I, uh, just have had a really awful night. And I would really like it to just be over.

(beat)

Can you help me? Please?

BEATRICE. How do I know you're really stuck?

DOVE. What?

BEATRICE. How do I know you're really –

DOVE. Why would I fake being stuck in the toilet?

BEATRICE. To trick me. Maybe you are rapist?

DOVE. Stuck in the toilet?

BEATRICE. Rapists can get stuck in toilets.

DOVE. I'm not a rapist.

BEATRICE. How do I know?

DOVE. Because, if I were a rapist and was trying to trick you, don't you think I would have just faked being stuck and already jumped you by now. Or better yet just waited near the door for you to turn the lights on instead of lying face down on the bathroom floor in the shitter!

BEATRICE. I didn't say you were smart rapist.

DOVE. *(yelling)* I'm not a rapist!

BEATRICE. Don't yell.

DOVE. *(quietly)* I am not a rapist.

BEATRICE. Then how come you knew all those ways to trick me. All those rapist plans with the faking and the pouncing. That's pretty rapist way of thinking. Or are you just sicko?

DOVE. I, I, I don't know what to tell you.

BEATRICE. And…you don't want me to call the police.

DOVE. I would really prefer not to have my picture on the front page of the Post: "One Armed Man Makes Number 2".

BEATRICE. Your arm is stuck?

DOVE. *(beat)* Yes.

BEATRICE. In toilet?

DOVE. *(beat)* Yes.

BEATRICE. How far?

DOVE. Far enough.

BEATRICE. How did you get your arm stuck in toilet?

(pause)

DOVE. It's a long story. Can you please help me now?

(She approaches the stall, quietly picks up the mop.)

BEATRICE. You stay where you are Mr. Maybe Rapist.

(She pushes open the door with the mop handle. **DOVE** *is stuck in the toilet practically up to his shoulder.)*

BEATRICE. My God, you're practically up to your shoulder.

DOVE. Yes, I realize this.

BEATRICE. How did you –

DOVE. Do you want money? I'll pay you. I only have thirty-six dollars on me now, but I can write you a check.

BEATRICE. *(backing away)* What do you take me for, some sort of prostitute, midnight maid schtup girl!

DOVE. Oh Christ! For the last time I am not a rapist, and I don't want to have sex with you, I just want to get my arm out of the toilet. *Now would you please give me some goddamn help!*

BEATRICE. You don't want to?

DOVE. What?

BEATRICE. Sex. I'm not so attractive.

DOVE. I haven't seen you. *(beat)* But you have very nice... feet.

BEATRICE. I know you don't want to have the sex with me. I know. You don't think I do, but I do. I know.

DOVE. Look I –

BEATRICE. I see, I have eyes. I know I'm not so, not...not like the others. I see. I see how I don't get looks when I walk by on the street. Not like the real women, with their flowy hair and their pretty make-up, and their full lips. Even if I put that college broth in my lips.

DOVE. What?

BEATRICE. College Inn chicken broth. From grocery store. For Meg Ryan lips.

DOVE. Collagen. It's collagen.

BEATRICE. Ya. I said. Even with college-inn, I'd still be transparent. Like a window. Like a window with thick lips. You look through and pay no attention, just interested in what's past it. I see too. I like to look at the real women too. I just don't...like to be in the way. So don't think that I don't know, cause I do, and please don't swear and yell anymore.

(She sobs. Some noise comes from inside the stall. A roll of toilet paper unravels across the floor. It bumps into her feet.)

DOVE. Sorry.

(She sits down and rips off some paper to dry her eyes.)

DOVE. I was supposed to meet my girlfriend for dinner. At nine. We were celebrating. She had just discovered this whole Native American circle of life thing and decided it was okay to eat meat and stop being a vegetarian, as long as you said a prayer of thanks over your steak. Hence, Peter Luger's Steak House. Anyway, I had been doing a lot of thinking lately and I decided that she was the best I was ever going to get. So I went out today and bought...

BEATRICE. A ring.

DOVE. A turtle. And a ring. On our first date, we went out to this chi-chi French restaurant and had turtle soup.

BEATRICE. This was before she was vegetarian?

DOVE. No, she was a vegetarian then, she was just never very good at it. Anyway, I thought it would be funny to begin her new omnivorous life with her now-sanctioned food source as a pet. So I put the ring around the turtle's neck, put the turtle in a small white box, and wrapped the box with a pink ribbon.

BEATRICE. That's very romantic.

DOVE. I thought so, but then I also once gave a girl a jar of dirt for an anniversary and told her it was the ground from where we first kissed. Anyway, to make a long story short –

BEATRICE. She never showed up.

DOVE. Six martinis later, at ten till closing, the turtle and I received a note from the maitre'de. Dear Dove, that's my name, Dove. What's yours?

BEATRICE. Beatrice. Bee for short.

DOVE. Pretty name.

BEATRICE. I always hated it.

DOVE. Right…Anyway, "Dear Dove, sorry to do this like this, but I met a Navaho man called, Sleeps with Eyes Shut, and we're moving to the Dakotas. All my apologies, love Jezebel."

BEATRICE. *(beat)* Der vas no note for true?

DOVE. *(sighs)* No. There was no note for true. Just a phone call, from my place. She wasn't meeting me, she had moved all her stuff out.

BEATRICE. You must feel awful.

DOVE. Yeah, I guess. I don't know how I feel really. Stunned mostly. She, uh, said I've been on autopilot for too long. I guess we're not– we weren't very good copilots. Funny, though, we looked so good on paper together.

BEATRICE. Even good paper gives cuts.

DOVE. No, I meant…

BEATRICE. I know, I know. Metafora.

DOVE.. Yeah, yeah. Metafora.

BEATRICE. Not so good.

DOVE. No. *(mimicking her accent)* Not so good.

BEATRICE. But how did you…

DOVE. Ah yes, I thought you had guessed. Well, I was crushed, and furious, and drunk. So I stormed into the bathroom, and…

BEATRICE. No!

DOVE. Yes.

BEATRICE. No.

DOVE. Yes!

BEATRICE. No.

> *(A white box with a pink ribbon trailing flies over the stall door and lands at her feet.)*

DOVE. Yes. So there I was, staring down into the porcelain well of my life, a peculiar soup of a small live paddling turtle and a diamond ring, when I had a moment of clarity.

BEATRICE. The turtle.

DOVE. The ring. I've only made one payment on it and have many, many more to go. So I quickly bent over and reached down for it when, much to my surprise –

BEATRICE. The infrared automatic flusher.

DOVE. The infrared automatic flusher. And that my kind lady is how I ended up with my arm stuck in a toilet.

BEATRICE. *(Beat)* Okay, we try get you out.

> *(She stands up, approaches his feet, picks them up and pulls with all her might. He isn't budging.)*

DOVE. Harder. Harder.

BEATRICE. Suck it in, suck it in.

DOVE. I can't I've still got the turtle.

BEATRICE. *(dropping legs)* You still have turtle?

DOVE. Well of course. He's got the ring. It's three carats!

BEATRICE. You have to...to let it go.

DOVE. No.

BEATRICE. Yes.

DOVE. No.

BEATRICE. Yes.

DOVE. No.

BEATRICE. Fine. Then you be stuck forever. So, just close your eyes again and sleep. Who knows, maybe girl-friend will come back and find you with arm stuck in toilet and you will get married in restaurant bathroom. Very romantic. Or, maybe she see you and remember why she left in first place. Because you are idiota with arm stuck in toilet.

DOVE. I'm not an idiota. I'm just trying to save a small fortune.

BEATRICE. Ya, ya, expensive American ring. I see. You don't see you already saved so much.

DOVE. What?

BEATRICE. It cost much more to marry wrong girl and have to pay for big divorce. Lawyer, house, car, paying her the all-the-money –

DOVE. Alimony?

BEATRICE. Yeah, all-the-money. Could have been worse. You could have flush life down toilet by marrying wrong girl. Your life worth much more than diamond ring, no?

DOVE. Well, yes...but...

BEATRICE. Your choice. Let go of ring and find better wife, or be stuck in shit bowl for rest of life. I have the work to do.

DOVE. No, wait. Don't go. You can't leave me here like this.

BEATRICE. Look, Mr. Buddy. I try to pull you out. I try to talk cents to you, but you only think of dollars. I have job to do.

DOVE. No, please, one more time.

BEATRICE. Let it go.

DOVE. I…I…I can't.

BEATRICE. You can.

(entering stall completely)

You're all flushed. What? Why you looking at me like that?

DOVE. My God…you're…so…

(She scoffs and dries him off with some paper towels.
DOVE screams in pain. She screams startled.)

BEATRICE. You're free.

DOVE. Oh thank god. Thank you.

BEATRICE. *(She helps him up and out of stall.)* For what? I did nothing. You let go.

DOVE. *(besotted and still touching)* Because of you.

BEATRICE. *(embarrassed)* I'm sorry you lost ring.

DOVE. *(still besotted)* It's…It's okay.

(He moves his wet arm to touch her and screams in pain.
She screams startled.)

DOVE. *(referring to his wet arm)* Pins and needles! Pins and needles!

BEATRICE. You shouldn't yell.

(She exits.)

DOVE. *(following)* Sorry.

(Pause. The toilet flushes. A small object drops from the
toilet to the floor. It is the turtle. He walks offstage.)

THE END

THE KING OF ROCK 'N' ROLL

By Richard Schotter

CHARACTERS

Alan Freed

Howie Golden

The premiere of *THE KING OF ROCK 'N' ROLL* was sponsored by The Jewish Theatre of New England. The production was directed by Judy Eraha, stage managed by Eileen Kelly, with Rock & Roll research by Tim Riley and the following cast:

ALAN FREED . . . . Ken Cheeseman
HOWIE GOLDEN . . . . Tasso Feldman

*(AT RISE: Lights up on a bedroom in a fifties era apartment in the Bronx. 1950's slow rock plays. A boy of fifteen, **HOWIE GOLDEN**, reluctantly picks up the telephone and dials.)*

HOWIE. Hello? Is this Allegra? *(beat)* It's Howie Golden. From World History. Third period. *(beat)* So. How you doing? Good. Me too. *(beat)* Listen, Allegra. There's this movie Saturday night at the Loew's Paradise. I thought, maybe, you and I…might… *(beat)* Oh, Really? A dance recital? *(beat)* Yeah. I understand. Maybe some other time. Well…Goodbye, see you in World History. Third period. *(hangs up phone, dejected)*

VOICE. *(off)* Have no fear, Howie. She'll be your sugar baby soon.

HOWIE. Who's that?

VOICE. This is Alan Freed. The King of Rock 'n' Roll.

HOWIE. It can't be. The radio isn't on.

VOICE. I'm not on the radio, Howie. I'm coming to you live in your bedroom. This portion of our conversation brought to you by the people at Friendly Frost.

HOWIE. This is amazing. I listen to your show every Saturday, Mr. Freed.

VOICE. I read the letter you sent me.

HOWIE. You did? Wow!

VOICE. You can't blame your parents if they're afraid of rock 'n' roll. They think it leads to sex, reefers, juvenile delinquency, communism. But we know better.

HOWIE. I can't believe this. The King of Rock 'n' Roll. In my bedroom. I'm about to send away for tickets for the Christmas show at the Brooklyn Paramount.

VOICE. Don't forget to buy the souvenir program.

HOWIE. And I was planning to ask a certain Allegra Goldstein to go with me.

VOICE. You're infatuated with this Allegra Goldstein?

HOWIE. Not infatuated. In love. Have you ever seen her?

VOICE. Can't say I have. But I've eaten dinner with Connie Francis. Lovely girl.

HOWIE. Allegra's the most beautiful girl in the world.

VOICE. She's sweet. And quite petite. When she walks into the room, she sweeps you off your feet.

HOWIE. Exactly. I asked her out.

VOICE. And she left you cryin' lonely teardrops. Try again. But this time, summon your rock 'n' roll soul. Every girl wants a boy with a rock 'n' roll soul.

HOWIE. You think I have one?

VOICE. Of course. You've just got to find it. And I've come to help you.

(ALAN *enters. He's a rather sleazy-looking man in his forties wearing a loud, brocade suit, a pinky ring, his hair slicked back. An anxious manner.*)

ALAN. This portion of our conversation is brought to you by the friendly folks at your Shopwell supermarket. This week featuring rib lamb chops at ninety-nine cents a pound.

HOWIE. Mr. Freed. It really is you. Can I offer you a beverage? Dr. Pepper? Orange Crush?

ALAN. No thanks. I'm trying to get the good folks at Coca Cola to be our sponsor. But more about that next week. Right now, we're working on your rock 'n' roll soul. Once you find it, it'll take you over the mountain, across the sea to find the treasure of love. And then this...Alexis.

HOWIE. ...Allegra.

ALAN. Will say to you, in the immortal words of Robert and Johnny, "Your mine, and we belong together." You see, Howie, when a girl senses a rock 'n' roll soul, she becomes your party doll, your Peggy Sue, your Sweet Little Sixteen, your Bony Maronie, Long Tall Sally, Coney Island Baby. Ooh, mama, ooh. We're rockin' now.

HOWIE. Jeez, Mr. Freed. You sound just like you do on the radio. What do I do? Send away my box tops? Coupons?

ALAN. First, you'll need my brand-new Alan Freed's Best Rock 'n' Roll Hits.

(Magically, **ALAN** *hands* **HOWIE** *a record.)*

HOWIE. Where'd that come from?

ALAN. My personal collection. Go on, Howie. Spin that disk. Cut number five.

*(***HOWIE*** puts on record. We hear Gene Vincent's "Bee-Bop- A-Lula."*)*

Did you hear the heartache, the pain, the longing? That's the rock 'n' roll soul, daddy-O. I'm gonna give that to you. Remember, Howie. Nothing matters but the music. They try to get me to play cover records by Pat Boone, the McGuire Sisters and I say no. The kids have to hear the real thing by the real artists. Black or white, it doesn't matter. What's important is the music. The music and the kids! *(beat)* Are you ready to free your rock 'n' soul?

HOWIE. You bet I am.

ALAN. Then we'll start the count down now. Try this on.

(A black leather jacket floats down from up above and lands near **HOWIE.***)*

HOWIE. Wow. That was something.

ALAN. I've got a million tricks up my sleeve.

HOWIE. I can't wear this.

ALAN. Why not?

HOWIE. The Fordham Baldies wear these. If they catch me, they'll beat me to a pulp.

ALAN. A boy must take risks for rock 'n' roll. Put on the jacket... *(***HOWIE*** does)* Good. Now look at yourself in the mirror.

HOWIE. *(approaches mirror awkwardly. Looks)* I don't know...

*See Music Use Note on Page 3

ALAN. I want you to inhabit that jacket. Make it your cloak of love. *(beat)* Ooh, poppa do. I've got an itchy twitchy feeling you're changing already. I see in you…a great lover.

HOWIE. Are you sure you got the right address?

ALAN. The King of Rock 'n' Roll always has the right address. *(beat)* How do you feel in the jacket?

HOWIE Kinda like a sausage.

ALAN. These'll make you feel better. *(A pair of black motorcycle boots slide in.)*

HOWIE. I can't wear these.

ALAN. *(beat)* They belonged to the late, great Johnny Ace. They have taps, toes and heels. When you walk, I want to hear the beat of your cold, metallic heart. Now, put them on and strut your way across the room like you're doing the stroll, the bop, the slide, the peppermint twist.

HOWIE. *(He tries, nothing.)* I don't think Allegra's gonna go for this.

ALAN. If you believe it, so will she. *(beat)* I'm sending this out to all the kids on Sheridan Avenue. To Tommy and Rita and Antoinette and Carl going steady three weeks. Do it, Howie. Not just for your Alexis…

HOWIE. Allegra.

ALAN. But for all the kids in our WINS listening area. They want to hear the music that makes them shimmy and shake like an old rattlesnake.

HOWIE. All right, Mr. Freed. I'll do it.

ALAN. That's what I like to hear. Now ready, set, go cat go! Let me see the Chuck Berry chicken walk, the Elvis sneer, the Jackie Wilson twirl. *(They do it.)* Yeah, baby yeah. Now we're really rockin'.

HOWIE. *(He tries, awkward.)* How'm I doing?

ALAN. Goodness gracious, great balls of fire! You're feeling it now. This time, add a heavy shot of rhythm and blues!

(Phone rings. HOWIE answers.)

HOWIE. Hello, Golden residence. Mr. Freed? Yeah. He's here. *(beat)* Mr. Freed. It's for you.

ALAN. This is Alan Freed, the King of Rock 'n' Roll. *(anxious)* Now? Impossible. You said you'd give me some warning. Tomorrow? All right. I'll be there. Nine o'clock. Federal Building. *(hangs up, upset)* Bastards.

HOWIE. What is it, Mr. Freed?

ALAN. Something's come up. *(takes out a flask, takes a quick nip)* Ovaltine. For quick energy. Pick it up at your local grocery store. Let's get back to your lessons in love.

HOWIE. We don't have to do this now, Mr. Freed. If you have other things on your mind.

ALAN. I made you a promise. I'll keep it. *(beat)* Audits, questions, inquisitions. For what, I ask you? A few dollars here. A few dollars there. Why don't they leave me alone?

HOWIE. Do you mean this payola thing, Mr. Freed?

ALAN. Don't say that word. Vultures. That's all they are. Preying on human flesh. I'm the man who coined the word the rock 'n' roll. They should be honoring me, not investigating me.

(Phone rings again. HOWIE picks it up.)

HOWIE. Golden residence. Mr. Freed? One minute. *(hands him phone)*

ALAN. Bernie. Yeah? What do they want now? *(beat)* No. They can't do that. They said they wouldn't bring them into it...

HOWIE. More trouble, Mr. Freed?

ALAN. A hunka, hunka, hunka trouble. I'm afraid we'll have to finish this another time.

HOWIE. I don't believe a word they say about you in the papers. You only play the songs you love. You said so. On the radio.

ALAN. That's right, Howie. And the songs I love make you feel good like a young boy should. They make you want to slow dance to the Platters and hang out on street corners singing harmonies that send chills up your spine with the radio ooh papa doo and Negro music and white music all shook up singing love round a microphone and the back beat, the back seat, the back beat pounding, and love and sweat – sweet, young sweat – and dancing forever with the kids rockin' on into the great American future. Ain't that right, daddy-O?

HOWIE. Yeah, Mr. Freed. You say it better than anyone.

ALAN. A rock 'n' roll kingdom. That's what it'll be. I might not get there with you, but I'll be happy knowing you're out there. Rockin'.

HOWIE. You' gotta get there with us, Mr. Freed. Before I listened to you, I was nothing but my parent's lonely son. But once I heard rock 'n' roll, real rock 'n' roll, the way only you play it, I realized there was a whole other world out there. A rock 'n' roll world. Just waitin' for me to grab it. It all came from the music, Mr. Freed. The music's your gift to us all.

ALAN. These government people don't understand rock 'n' roll. Before I go, I want you to know, you've got a rock 'n' roll soul.

(hands **HOWIE** *an envelope)*

HOWIE. What's this?

ALAN. Two tickets. Front row, center. Brooklyn Paramount. Buddy Holly will be there. Little Richard. Jerry Lee Lewis. All the gang. Bring your reet petite. Call her. Woo her.

HOWIE. I'll be listening Saturday morning.

ALAN. When I dedicate a song to Howie Golden, the boy with the rock 'n' roll soul. *(beat)* Maybe one day, when this is all over, people'll remember what I did for you kids.

HOWIE. You'll be famous, Mr. Freed. An American hero.

ALAN. *(beat)* And now, the old clock on the studio wall's saying it's time to go. *(begins to exit)*

HOWIE. Good-bye, Mr. Freed.

ALAN. Not good-bye, Howie. Good night. *(ALAN takes out flask, takes another nip, begins to leave.)* I'm sending this one out to all the kids at Abraham Lincoln High School. To Maddy and Ernie and Alvi and Buddy and Cherry and Estelle and Jerry and little Jerry and...

HOWIE. I'll never forget you. And what you've given me.

(ALAN leaves. HOWIE looks in the mirror, poses, struts, poses again. "Earth Angel" by the Penguins begins to play.* HOWIE goes to the phone, he dials.)

HOWIE. Hey, Allegra. Howie Golden here. How's it going? You're sounding good. Like a young girl should. *(beat)* Howie Golden. Remember? Listen something's come up. I just got these tickets. *(beat)* Tickets to what? Well, that's kind of...a long story.

BLACKOUT

*See Music Use Note on Page 3.

POP! – THE MUSICAL

By Sara Adelman Ring and Dan Ring

CHARACTERS

ESTHER FRYE – Soprano. Late teens/early twenties. Dreams of becomming a pop star.

MIKE – Baritone. Late teens/early twenties. Esther's long-suffering boyfriend and co-worker at the Dairy Queen.

THE MOGUL – Tenor. Mid thirties to late fifties. A sleazy music producer.

TANYA – Alto. Early to late twenties. A hip MTV Veejay.

SETTING

Although occuring in several different locations, sets for this piece can be minimal, with each setting being suggested rather than presented realistically.

TIME

The present.

Note: The play is entirely sung-through.

ACT I

(**ESTHER** *stands behind the counter of a Dairy Queen, dreamily reading through a* People Magazine.)

ESTHER.

MY LITTLE TOWN IS SO QUIET AND TAME
'CAUSE EVERY DAY HERE IS JUST THE SAME
AND SO I DAYDREAM OF WEALTH AND FAME
WOULDN'T YOU?
THEN I'M THE STAR OF THE STAGE AND SCREEN
THE COVER OF PEOPLE MAGAZINE
OKAY, SO I WORK AT THE DAIRY QUEEN
SAD BUT TRUE.

(**MIKE** *enters, sweeping the floor.*)

ESTHER. *(cont'd)*

MIKE, WOULDN'T YOU LIKE TO MAKE IT BIG?
BE WORSHIPPED AND ADORED?

MIKE.

ESTHER, FAME IS A LOUSY GIG
I'M SURE THAT I'D GET BORED.

ESTHER.

BUT WOULDN'T LIFE BE SO WICKED FUN –

MIKE.

– IF YOU'RE A FAMOUS STAR?

ESTHER.

I ONLY WANT TO BE SOMEONE.

MIKE.

BUT YOU ALREADY ARE.

ESTHER.

SO I'M A PRISONER OF CIRCUMSTANCE
NO ONE WOULD PAY ME TO SING AND DANCE
ALL THAT I ASK IS TO GET MY CHANCE!

(**THE MOGUL** *is passing by the store and hears* **ESTHER** *sing.*)

MOGUL.

MY GOD, DID THAT COME FROM HER?

ESTHER.

HOW CAN I HELP YOU, SIR?

MOGUL.

HELLO! I'D LIKE TO GET ONE POP STAR, TO GO!

ESTHER. Who're they?

MOGUL.

WELL, WHO ARE YOU?

ESTHER.

I'M ESTHER FRYE!

MOGUL.

THAT SUCKS! FROM NOW ON YOU'RE – SKYE!
AND SO WE'RE FAME AND FORTUNE-BOUND
YOU'LL LEAVE THAT LOSER AND THIS HUM-DRUM
TOWN
THINK WHAT YOU COULD BE AND FORGET WHO
YOU ARE
'CAUSE I AM GONNA MAKE YOU

ESTHER.

HE IS GONNA MAKE ME!

MOGUL.

I AM GONNA MAKE YOU A STAR!

(**TANYA** *appears stage right, giving an on-air report into a microphone.*)

TANYA.

YO, WHAT'S UP, THIS IS TANYA FROM MTV
BRINGING YOU THE SCOOP ON CELEBRITY
THERE'S A NEW KID IN TOWN, AND WE HEAR SHE'S
FLY
SHE'S REACHING FOR THE STARS AND HER NAME IS
SKYE.

MOGUL.

WE'RE SO CLOSE, BUT I STILL CAN'T TELL
EXACTLY WHO WE'RE TRYING TO SELL

(He puts a cowboy hat on her head.)

Try country.

ESTHER. *(singing country-western style)*
BOY I KNOW YOU WANT IT
GOT NO NEED TO FLAUNT IT
GET IT WHILE THE GETTIN' IS GOOD.

(sees the Mogul's displeased expression)

No?

MOGUL. No.

*(**ESTHER** takes off the cowboy hat.)*

TANYA.
HER FUTURE'S SO BRIGHT, NO SHADES CAN DIM IT
FOR THIS NEW STAR, THE SKY'S THE LIMIT.

MOGUL. *(putting a boa around her neck)* How 'bout jazz?

ESTHER. *(sings in a jazzy style)*
BOY, I KNOW YOU WANT IT
GOT NO NEED TO FLAUNT IT
BETTER GET IT WHILE THE GETTING IS GOOD.
SCOOBY-DO-WAAAA!

MOGUL. No.

*(**ESTHER** takes off the boa.)*

TANYA.
SHE'S LIVING THE HIGH LIFE WITH WADS OF MONEY
YOU KNOW HER SKIES ARE ALWAYS SUNNY.

MOGUL. *(putting a black wool cap on her head)* Let's try a post-Seattle, neo-grunge, indie garage rock!

ESTHER. *(screaming)*
BOY! I KNOW YOU WANT IT!

MOGUL. *(interrupting)* For the love of God, no!

*(**ESTHER** takes off the cap.)*

TANYA.
SO SKYE IS THE POP WORLD'S NEXT BIG THING
SHE'S A STAR AND WE HAVEN'T EVEN HEARD HER SING!

BUT THAT'S ABOUT TO CHANGE, 'CAUSE TONIGHT YOU'LL SEE
SKYE'S DEBUT PERFORMANCE HERE ON MTV!

(TANYA and THE MOGUL exit. ESTHER takes center stage for her performance at the MTV Music Awards.)

ESTHER.

Uh!

I got it all right here, baby.

So come get it.

BOY, I KNOW YOU WANT IT
GOT NO NEED TO FLAUNT IT
GET IT WHILE THE GETTING'S GOOD
AH, AH, AH
LET ME SEE YOU SHAKE IT
I KNOW WE CAN MAKE IT
TAKE IT LIKE YOU KNOW THAT YOU SHOULD
BABY, TELL ME WHEN YOU'RE READY
IT'S RIGHT HERE WAITING FOR YOU!
YOU CAN'T FIND WHAT YOU'RE LOOKING FOR
THERE'S AN ACHE THAT YOU CAN'T IGNORE
SEARCH NO MORE, 'CAUSE I'VE GOT THE CURE
AND THE ANSWER'S CLEAR
I GOT IT ALL RIGHT HERE
HERE
HERE!

(BLACK OUT)

(Lights up on ESTHER in her dressing room after the performance.)

ESTHER.

MY LITTLE TOWN WAS A GIANT BORE
NOW I HAVE ALL THAT I WANT AND MORE
DID WHAT I HAD TO AND SO I CAN'T REGRET IT
WHY CAN'T I FORGET IT?

(MIKE tentatively enters, carrying a rose.)

MIKE.

DOES THE POP STAR HAVE A MINUTE OR TWO?

ESTHER.

OH, MIKE, AM I EVER GLAD TO SEE YOU.

MIKE.

I'VE MISSED YOU, ESTHER.

ESTHER.

I'VE MISSED YOU, TOO

IN FACT, THERE'S SOMETHING THAT I NEED TO SAY
TO YOU...

*(***THE MOGUL*** barges in, ignoring* **MIKE.***)*

MOGUL.

SKYE, YOU'RE A HIT, YOU'RE THE LATEST CRAZE

NOW HERE'S THE PLAN FOR THE NEXT THREE DAYS

TALK TO LETTERMAN IN BETWEEN *COSMO* AND
SEVENTEEN

FOLLOWED BY *PEOPLE* MAGAZINE.

STOP IN KANSAS, NEVADA, AND MAINE FOR THREE
CONCERTS

MEET OUR FRIENDS AT SKY VODKA, OUR CORPORATE
SPONSORS

THAT'S ONLY THREE DAYS AND YOU'RE ANXIOUS, I
KNOW

BUT YOU'RE YOUNG AND YOU'RE TIRED

SO WE'RE TAKING IT SLOW.

*(***TANYA*** barges in with her microphone and immediately
begins interrogating* **ESTHER.** **MIKE** *slinks off-stage.)*

TANYA.

HOW'S THE NEW KID ON THE BLOCK?

MTV'S CRÈME DE LA CRÈME?

IS IT TRUE THAT YOU DATED FRED DURST

DUMPING P. DIDDY FIRST

WHILE YOU SLEPT WITH EMINEM?

THESE AREN'T HARD QUESTIONS, YOU'LL CONCEDE

AND A MOMENT LIKE THIS IS WHAT YOU NEED

PLEASE TELL YOUR FANS WHO YOU ARE, WHAT'S
THE DEAL?

ARE YOU SCARED? HOW'S YOUR HEALTH?

DO YOU EAT? ARE THOSE REAL?

WON'T YOU LOOK IN THE CAMERA AND SAY HOW
YOU FEEL
TO BE UP ON THE TOP?
TO BE UP ON THE TOP?
TO BE UP ON THE TOP?
TO BE UP ON THE TOP?

MOGUL. *(overlapping, beginning after "you'll concede")*
STOP IN KANSAS, NEVADA, AND MAINE FOR THREE
CONCERTS
MEET OUR FRIENDS AS SKY VODKA, OUR CORPORATE
SPONSORS
THAT'S ONLY THREE DAYS AND YOU'RE ANXIOUS, I
KNOW
BUT YOU'RE YOUNG AND YOU'RE TIRED
SO WE'RE TAKING IT SLOW.
NOW THE WHOLE WORLD IS WATCHING AND
LISTENING
'CAUSE YOU'RE UP ON THE TOP
'CAUSE YOU'RE UP ON THE TOP
'CAUSE YOU'RE UP ON THE TOP
'CAUSE YOU'RE UP ON THE TOP

ESTHER. *(Simultaneous with the final "up on the top")*
PLEASE JUST STOP!
NO MORE QUESTIONS
I'D LIKE TO BE LEFT ALONE.

(TANYA heads stage right to give her report. **ESTHER** *and*
THE MOGUL. *head stage left to his office, where* **ESTHER**
pours over a tabloid.)

TANYA.
YO, IT'S TANYA, HERE, AND I'M ON THE MARK
WHEN I TELL YOU ALL THE SKY'S GONE DARK
HISSY FITS AND A MELTDOWN TOSSED IN
SHE'S SUFFERING FROM "EXHAUSTION."

ESTHER.
I CAN'T BELIEVE ALL THIS BAD PRESS
I'M THE GIRL THEY LOVE TO HATE

TANYA.

MADE IT BIG, BUT CAN IT LAST?

THIS SHOOTING STAR IS FALLING FAST

MOGUL. *(looking over her shoulder at paper)*

THAT'S THE PRICE YOU PAY FOR YOUR SUCCESS,

AND HEY, YOUR HAIR LOOKS GREAT!

TANYA.

KEEPS TO HERSELF, SHE'S STRANGE AND SHY

A SECRET LIFE? IS SHE SKY-HIGH?

MOGUL.

YOUR RECORDS SALES ARE WORSE THAN SLOW

YOUR MOVIE WAS A BOMB

TANYA.

GAINED SOME WEIGHT AND GETTIN' DOWDY

LOOKS LIKE RAIN, SKY IS CLOUDY

MOGUL.

BUT I JUST BOOKED YOUR COMEBACK SHOW

THE PARK SCHOOL JUNIOR PROM!

TANYA.

CAN'T IGNORE WHEN FAILURE'S CALLIN'

THIS LITTLE CHICK SAYS THE SKY HAS FALLEN!

LIGHTS GO DOWN ON STAGE RIGHT

ESTHER.

I'M LEAVING!

MOGUL.

WHY? THIS IS WHAT YOU DREAMED OF.

ESTHER.

DON'T TRY TO ACT AS IF YOU GIVE A DAMN

I THOUGHT THAT I WANTED THE FAME,

BUT I JUST WANTED LOVE

YOU ONLY CARE WHAT I SELL

NOT WHO I AM.

MOGUL.

SO LEAVE, I'VE ALREADY SIGNED SOMEONE NEW

WHO WILL LOVE YOU NOW?

*(**MIKE** suddenly appears.)*

MIKE.

I DO.

ESTHER. Mike!

MIKE.

DOES THE POP STAR HAVE A MINUTE OR TWO?

(**THE MOGUL** *leaves in disgust.*)

MIKE.

SO JUST TELL ME WHEN YOU'RE READY
IT'S RIGHT HERE WAITING FOR YOU
YOU CAN'T FIND WHAT YOU'RE LOOKING FOR
THERE'S AN ACHE THAT YOU CAN'T IGNORE
SEARCH NO MORE 'CAUSE I'VE GOT THE CURE
AND THE ANSWER'S CLEAR

ESTHER. *(overlapping)*

I SEE IT IN YOU
YOU'RE ALL THAT I NEED
MIKE, I LOVE YOU
WE'LL NEVER BE APART AGAIN

MIKE.

YOU HAD IT ALL RIGHT HERE

ESTHER.

THIS IS ALL I'VE BEEN LOOKING FOR
TOGETHER
AND WE'LL HAVE IT ALL RIGHT HERE...

(*They run out of breath, take a deep breath in, and finish the note.*)

– EEEEEERE!

THE END

ADOPT A SAILOR

By Charles Evered

CHARACTERS

PATRICIA – A gallery owner
RICHARD – A college professor
SAILOR – A young E2 Seaman Apprentice

AUTHOR'S NOTE

Before being produced in Boston, *Adopt a Sailor* was premiered from September 9-11, 2002, during the Brave New World event at Town Hall in New York City. The play was directed by Craig Carlisle and starred (in a rotating cast) Neil Patrick Harris, Michael Nouri, Amy Irving, Anne Jackson, Bebe Neuwirth, Liev Schreiber, Eli Wallach and Sam Waterston.

*(**SETTING**: Patricia and Richard's finely appointed dining room in their Tribeca Co-op, New York City. A year after the attacks of 9/11.)*

*(**AT RISE**: **RICHARD** is seated at the table and the young **SAILOR** hovering near it uncomfortably. The table setting tells us dinner is over. The **SAILOR** is dressed in his dress whites, his green sea bag leaning against a table behind him. **PATRICIA** enters with an open bottle of wine in one hand and a full glass in the other.)*

PATRICIA. *(to* **SAILOR***)* All I have left is a Montrachet '97, is that okay?

SAILOR. It's fine with me, Ma'am.

RICHARD. Darling, I hardly think he's that picky. *(to* **SAILOR***)* No offense to you, of course. Not implying at all that you're not a connoisseur – it's just that I imagine you don't much obsess about vintage.

SAILOR. No Sir, not usually.

*(**PATRICIA** pours some in the **SAILOR**'s glass. The **SAILOR** sits.)*

SAILOR. Thank you, Ma'am.

PATRICIA. Oh, please, anything but Ma'am.

SAILOR. Sorry, Ma'am, I mean.

PATRICIA. Patricia.

SAILOR. "Patricia," right.

RICHARD. Is that something they drill into you early on?

SAILOR. Sir?

RICHARD. The by-rote response – the "Ma'am, Sir" retort. I imagine after awhile, it becomes reflexive.

SAILOR. Well, I'm not sure about that, sir. I just mean it as a sign of respect.

RICHARD. Of course.

SAILOR. I guess it's something I just got used to.

PATRICIA. *(to* **RICHARD***)* You're making him self-conscious.

RICHARD. And you're projecting.

PATRICIA. Why is it every observation I make that you feel uncomfortable with is a "projection," while every observation you make is an "insight?" Can you rectify that cavernous disparity for me?

RICHARD. I could, but now would hardly be the appropriate time or place.

SAILOR. *(indicating wine)* It's real good.

PATRICIA. I'm so glad you like it.

(**PATRICIA** *goes to sit. The* **SAILOR** *stands up.* **PATRICIA** *takes notice)*

PATRICIA. Oh my goodness.

SAILOR. Ma'am?

PATRICIA. Richard, he stood for me.

(**SHE** *sits.)*

RICHARD. So he did.

(The **SAILOR** *sits.)*

PATRICIA. Richard hasn't stood for me in years.

RICHARD. *(to* **SAILOR***)* Just ignore our little "spats." This is the way people talk when they don't love each other anymore.

SAILOR. Sir?

RICHARD. I was kidding, I was being sardonic.

SAILOR. Oh.

PATRICIA. Sardonic is what people become when they don't have the balls to be truthful anymore.

SAILOR. Boy, listening to you two is, it's like a tennis match, it really is, my neck is hurtin' just listening to you. Bouncing, bouncing, back and forth. I hope you'll forgive me. I'm just having a little trouble keeping up. You are both very smart people.

PATRICIA. Now, you're being sardonic.

SAILOR. No, Ma'am.

RICHARD. So what is the name of this week again?

SAILOR. "Fleet Week," sir.

RICHARD. Right, "Fleet Week."

PATRICIA. I just love it. All of you running around the city in your crisp, white uniforms. Craning up your necks.

RICHARD. You should like the uniforms. You pay for them.

PATRICIA. Oh, just ignore Richard. Richard is a humbug. Richard doesn't like the military very much.

(**PATRICIA** *pours herself another drink.*)

RICHARD. In defense of myself, that's not exactly true. It's the ethic. It's the military ethic I find myself somewhat opposed to.

PATRICIA. Oh, I think it's worse than that. I would say you were virulently anti-military. I think if the military were a race, that you would be a racist.

RICHARD. I think you're exaggerating just a tad, darling. *(to* **SAILOR***)* Please feel perfectly welcome. When Patricia told me she was "bringing home a sailor" – you could imagine it threw me for a little loop.

SAILOR. Yes, sir.

PATRICIA. It's a program, Richard. How many times do I have to tell you? "Adopt A Sailor." It's a program, and that's what it's called.

RICHARD. Well, regardless, it's not everyday your wife brings home a sailor. Or is it everyday, darling? Maybe this is just the first time you've told me about it.

PATRICIA. I don't think I'll respond to that.

SAILOR. *(starting to stand)* Maybe this isn't the best time –

PATRICIA. *(pushing him down)* Of course it is. Sit. *(to* **RICH-ARD***)* Susan adopted a sailor as well. She had hers yesterday.

RICHARD. Did she?

PATRICIA. That's where I heard about it. *(to* **SAILOR***)* Susan is my nearest and dearest. She was the one who showed me the flier with all the information about it. I just think it's the most adorable idea. And why shouldn't someone "adopt" you all while you're here protecting us. A hot meal, fresh laundry. We're just giving back. Someone to look after you while you're far away from home. She said that you were all going fast, and that if I wanted to reserve one of you I better act fast. And I did.

RICHARD. You make him sound like a sale at Saks.

PATRICIA. Well, it's adorable. It's an adorable little program and I'm glad to do it.

RICHARD. *(to* **SAILOR***)* "Adorable," if you haven't noticed, being the operative word.

PATRICIA. Susan is even sewing for the sailor she got. She's sewing a patch on his little sea-coat. Or jacket. Or pea jacket, whatever you call it.

RICHARD. Susan is sewing?

PATRICIA. Well, she's having someone else do it, but she arranged it.

RICHARD. *(to* **SAILOR***)* Warms the cuckolds, doesn't it?

SAILOR. Well, I certainly appreciate this, Ma'am. Whoops, sorry, I mean, "Patricia." The food, and all the nice table settings and stuff.

PATRICIA. Don't be silly. It's the least we can do, after all you do for us.

RICHARD. Ever since the tragedy last September, my wife has been living in a movie scored by Aaron Copeland.

SAILOR. Sir?

RICHARD. Actually, I've had a little military experience myself. Well, I suppose "military like" would be closer to the truth.

PATRICIA. You are not going to talk about what I think you're going to talk about, are you?

RICHARD. Well, why shouldn't I? It was "boot camp," wasn't it?

PATRICIA. "Academic Boot Camp."

RICHARD. Well, still, we got up early. And it was quite regimented. It was!

SAILOR. *(sincere)* Yes, sir.

RICHARD. I felt like, now of course, I don't know, but I felt like I was really in the military. We would have to write drafts of our dissertations or you know, whatever we were working on. It so happens at this time I was working on something comparing and contrasting the subjective models used in post modern methodology and how it related to post-colonial neo-Western thought. Or something along those lines.

SAILOR. Sir?

RICHARD. Which as you could imagine, was no cake walk.

SAILOR. No, sir.

RICHARD. Especially at the crack of nine every morning, when they would roust us from our little cots.

SAILOR. No, sir.

PATRICIA. This is so terribly embarrassing.

SAILOR. Were you both here?

PATRICIA. For what?

SAILOR. When the planes came in. Were you here?

RICHARD. You mean for the tragedy?

SAILOR. Sir?

PATRICIA. Oh, don't mind Richard. He's just deflecting. He and I don't quite see "eye to eye" on this. If we did, he wouldn't use the banal and neutral term "tragedy" to describe the attacks. If the word "tragedy" were a country, it would be Switzerland.

RICHARD. Are you implying it wasn't a tragedy?

PATRICIA. The sinking of the Titanic was a tragedy. What happened last September was a calculated heinous crime. An atrocity. An act of war. An attack. Hear that, city! An attack! *(to* **SAILOR***)* If you live in the boroughs, you can call it an attack. If you live down here or on the Upper West Side and call it an "attack" – you're a fascist war mongerer. "Attack" is too accusatory. It implies fault on the part of the attacker or whoops, I should say "perpetuator" of said "incident." It was an "occurrence" and nothing more. That's the party line anyway.

RICHARD. *(to* SAILOR*)* You'll have to forgive her. My wife is intent on ignoring what anyone with even an elementary grasp of geopolitical confluences might call "underlying causes." To her, this came out of the blue. To those of us with a little more, breadth of scope, it's simply icing on a cake left unattended years ago.

PATRICIA. *(to* SAILOR*)* It's my husband you should forgive. Somehow Richard and his friends up at Columbia believe that if we have a foreign policy that favors Israel – rich, sexually repressed Saudi frat boys should have the right to indiscriminately kill fellow Muslims working at Windows on the World for six dollars an hour.

RICHARD. Oh, quaint.

PATRICIA. *(to* SAILOR*)* Following his logic, a woman who gets raped is "asking for it" because she happens to be wearing fishnet stockings. I find that a strange and even contradictory viewpoint for a dyed-in-the-wool liberal to have, don't you?

RICHARD. Disingenuous to the core.

PATRICIA. The problem of course, is that he didn't see it happen. Not live anyway. Not with his own eyes, as it was happening. That's what changed my thinking. That's the difference between me and Richard. And it always will be.

RICHARD. Here it comes.

PATRICIA. Well, it's true. *(to* SAILOR*)* I was supposed to open the gallery early that day, but I was running late. I was out on the terrace watering the plants when I heard it at first, the engine. The engine of the first plane. He was flying it straight down the Hudson. They say he was following the river to navigate his way down to the towers. Of course when I saw him fly over, I knew something was awfully wrong right away. Planes just don't fly that close to buildings. Not over New York anyway. Maybe Hong Kong, but not in New York. "Something is out of whack," I thought, because his wings were dipping a little. And the sound of the engine. Something was strange about it. It didn't sound right. Someone told me later it was because "what's his name," the little twerp flying the first one, what was his name? "Atta?" He didn't really know how to fly it. It was in the wrong gear, or whatever you call it on planes. And there I saw it, right in front of me. Him, dipping it down and puttering it, almost puttering the plane into the building and I remember thinking how strange it was that I was seeing it happen, but not hearing it. But you know, it takes awhile for the sound wave or the shock wave or whatever you call it and I just stood there. I don't even think I screamed. "I must be in a dream," I thought. What I saw must be a dream. Or maybe it was television. "This must be television I'm watching," I thought, because it was too real to be real. And I remember picking up my cell phone and calling 911, can you imagine how ridiculous? As though I would be the first caller. As though no one else would think to call. "A plane just flew into the…" I even forget what it was I said to the operator. "A plane just…" And then I called Richard and he had a class.

RICHARD. A department meeting actually.

PATRICIA. A department meeting, right. And so I just stood there. With my hand over my mouth. And then the second one. That was different. Straight in. That bastard knew what he was doing, oh yeah. I always think now, how elated he must have been, the bastard flying that one. How elated he must have been to see the other tower on fire. It must have been like a big green light to him. A big "how do ya do!" A big happy handshake. Him, I imagine smiling while he rammed it in. The little children on board with their parents, and the parents trying to calm them down, right up to the last minute, trying to explain why it was they were flying so close to the buildings. Yeah, I'll bet you anything he was smiling when he rammed that one in.

(Pause. **PATRICIA** *refills her glass.)*

RICHARD. It was an awful, awful day.

PATRICIA. I cried. I cried for days straight. Days.

SAILOR. *(to* **PATRICIA,** *earnest)* I'm very sorry.

PATRICIA. Thank you. *(pause)* Richard on the other hand.

RICHARD. Patricia.

PATRICIA. Richard and his comrades up at Columbia had a little bit of a different response.

RICHARD. You're embarrassing yourself.

PATRICIA. They had "forums." "Panels." Oh, it was hilarious. You should have seen them all. All these baby boomer half men with their middle age paunches and co-ed girlfriends hanging on their every word. And their Vietnam deferments still rankling their puny psyches. "Forums and Panels," every other ridiculous pointless day. Why we deserved it. Why we deserved to have planes flown into our buildings.

RICHARD. *(to* **SAILOR***)* See, this is what I meant by her inability to –

PATRICIA. No, no, no, Richard, THIS – THIS Richard, is how people talk when they don't love each other anymore.

(Long silence. Slowly, the **SAILOR** *gets up)*

SAILOR. Well, I, I better get…

(The **SAILOR** *moves toward his duffle bag, slings it over his shoulder. Turns back to* **RICHARD** *and* **PATRICIA.***)*

SAILOR. Well I, I really do appreciate, you both are too smart for me. I must have just sat there boring you. I'm sorry about that. I'm just a, sometimes down in the galley, you know, they'll have the talk shows on, you know, the news ones on Sunday mornings and I'll just look up at 'em, ya know, and I'll marvel at the, not that I don't understand them, I do. I had a year or so of college. Not a big one like Columbia, but, but I think it's great the talks you must have up there. I think it's good to talk about it. I do, really. Maybe by your talking about it, maybe stuff like what happened won't happen again. I admire you for it, I really do. (RICHARD *looks at him.*) As for me, I wish I could see things that complicated but I was out in the middle of the Indian Ocean when it happened. I remember we saw it on the television and then that night I had watch again, as usual, out on deck and I remember looking up and sure enough, seeing every star out that night that I saw the night before. Stupid, I know, but that's what I was thinking. What with all that just happened that day, all the awfulness and all the meanness and the evil that they tried to do to us, every star I saw the night before was still right up there. And I thought, "That's good. That's a good thing." And it was beautiful that night. Just a beautiful, beautiful star filled night.

(RICHARD *and* PATRICIA *remain perfectly still.*)

SAILOR. Anyway, I...I sure do appreciate....

(The SAILOR *turns, goes to the door and opens it. He turns back, puts his cap on and tips it a little toward them, smiling sweetly. He closes the door behind him.* PATRICIA *gets up, takes a few steps toward the door, then stops. She looks back toward* RICHARD. *He looks back at her as the lights slowly fade to black.)*

THE END

AMEREKA

By Ronan Noone

CHARACTERS

Man

*(This is a **MAN** around fifty years of age. He speaks in an 'Eastern European' accent. He wears a white short sleeved shirt. The top two buttons are open revealing a little cross. He has an American flag pin fastened to the shirt. He wears a grey pants with soft black loafers. He smiles gently with an appreciation for life and when he uses the word 'Yes' it is in a defeated way. There are two chairs on the stage each with the wooden car seat rack tied on to them. Lights come up on the man, who is at the back of the stage, with a wet sponge in his hand. He looks tired but strong. He drops the wet sponge and walks towards the chair. He takes out his keys and opens the imaginary door to the driver seat and sits in. He looks out the windscreen and waits before talking.)*

MAN. I lovf Amereka. I do. I lovf Amereka. I live here ten years now and everything is here. I take the lessons to drive and I get my license here.

Big Policeman who do the test, shake my hand, congratulate me, and I am delighted. My wife and me celebrate. Big day. Well, small big day.

I buy my first car in here. This car. Ford Taurus, like the bull. My wife says I get the car because I am like a bull. She's crazy. "Get out my kitchen you bull." I laugh. She laughs. She likes the car. Yes.

I sit in the car for ten minutes every morning that to admire outside from it, and smile at people going by. I turn it on and let it run for maybe three – six minutes, maybe longer in the cold.

I turn on the radio. World news. I listen – I turn volume, up down how I like. My neighbours they know all my car. Then I stop engine off. I lock secure. I get the bus to work.

When I buy it my wife she was there. I ask her what colour she would like and she says blue. And I said blue and the man of the sales say we only have blue.

Blue. Yes. I got automatic for easier to drive. And I bought wooden rack for to sit on, make the seat more comfortable and one for my wife too. *(looks to the passenger seat)* You call accessory. My first car accessory. It gives you relieved.

We drive around every Sunday on the highway to Concord to see the peaceful lake of the writer. And then we wash the car together when we come home. Lots of water.

Last month ago I came out of my house and I see scrape all along the side of the blue. Done by nail, or key, or pin, or screwdriver I don't know.

My wife calm me down and, but I am bad. I can say because you work hard you can buy a car. That is this country. So I start to watch my car every night from our apartment so I can see who would do such a thing.

My wife calls me to the bed and I say soon and she says I'm crazy. But I was afraid. "It is only a car," she says and we fight.

(loudly) This car is my first car. I learn to drive here. All my first money is the car. It takes us to everywhere we want go, no problem. I drive this car to the Fanueil hall where they make the proud speech.

Where the music orchestra play God Bless Amereka and we put our right hand in the air and said Oath of Allegiance. I pledge Allegiance to the flag of the U-nite-ted States of Amereka. Off by my heart I know this.

And to the Republic for which it stands; one nation under God, in-de-vis-e-bull with liberty and justice for all.

I change my last name to shorter Amerecan version that day. Four hundred people, three hundred and fifty people change their name, no problem. You too.

We drive to the restaurant and had the dinner and I said I am glad to be Amerecan and you agree with me.

(calmer) She went to bed. Yes. Five nights I wait by the window and then I see this boy maybe sixteen, eighteen and he is trying to break the side mirror from the car for no why.

I shout to my wife and I rush out. I shout to my wife – I come at him, but he runs like chicken, and I see the mirror broken down by the side and get more mad like a bull now.

I breath like bull, never have I been this mad before, not here, I chase and I chase, not once am I tired, I just chase, and he turns down alley road, and he is trapped - and I beat him.

I beat him bad and I say to him. I am American. I live here. My home is here. I am citizen of here. Why?

I leave him in bundle like roll in rain water on the road, crying, and I walk home. I see my wife wait on the doorstep and we look at the car and we are both sad. I catch my breath.

This was not right. She puts arm around my shoulder and I said, I beat him. I beat him good, and she says, he will not be back. Yes.

I try to stick the black tape on the mirror to the car to keep in place and den two big policeman come to me, ask me my name and I said yes, and they say;

Did I beat up young man tonight and I say, I say look at my car, this mirror he break and he scrape the blue from the side. They arrest me and I tell my wife not to worry. They put me in the jail.

My wife come pay one thousand dollars to get me out. One thousand dollars. And when I get home next morning I sit in my car, I turn engine on and I wait to see.

Yes. Den I went for drive to the lake for some peace, and I hear the mirror bang off the side so I have to stop the car and drive slowly home. I didn't want anymore destruction.

I work a little harder that week. I make some more money to fix the paint and the mirror and I buy a secure big steel lock for steering wheel. Another accessory for to make me better and everything safer.

Seven hundred thirty two dollars fifty six cents. But it look good as new. My wife said I should not have spend it on this because we would need it. The lawyer said I may go to the jail.

But I want the car to be good looking, for her, for me and for my neighbours for when they look out their window they could see everything is here and it is good.

In the court the judge give me the suspended sentence. *(blesses himself)* There is justice in that. That is Amereka too.

So I was glad. And I kiss my wife. I saw the man, boy, in the court I beat, and he had broken arm and bandage on his face and big jewelry cross on his chest. Accessory.

I was wrong I say. Where I come from it was right but not here. And I apologise. He say nothing.

I walk home, and when I get home I went to my car and I give it wash. Everything. I sat in my car. I was relieve. I look out window then I lock big steel lock and I smile.

I smile now. I say goodnight to my Ford Taurus Bull. Yes.

(Gets out of the chair and closes the door. Locks it with the key. Goes back and picks up the dripping sponge and turns around.)

Goodnight Ford Taurus Bull.

(Blackout.)

SMURF

By John Kuntz

CHARACTERS

Pearl

*(AT RISE: Lights up on empty chair. **PEARL**, an elderly woman, enters walking towards her chair, center.)*

PEARL. Alright. Alright...here I come. *(to the interviewer)* Don't move! If you move, you'll step in something. *(to Boris)* Boris, stop that! *(to the interviewer)* Can I get you something? Coffee? *(to Nadine, admonishingly)* Nadine... *(to the interviewer)* How about a Snapple soda? Would you like a Snapple soda? I have some Snapple soda... *(to two fighting cats)* Don't make me come over there, you two. *(to the interviewer)* No? Well, all right...

(She sits, straightens her dress and smiles.)

Well. First of all, let me say that I am absolutely thrilled to be interviewed for *Cat Fancy* Magazine. I feel this is one of the pinnacles... *(to a cat clawing at her feet, slapping him away)* DOWN! *(to the interviewer)* ...of my life. Yes, that's right. I have 258 cats and I love them all. I feed them, take care of them, they all have names... Of course, by the time this article is published I might only have 257 cats if you don't stop eating that... *(She swings suddenly to her left, to Jasper)* ...FERN, JASPER! Jasper, you eat that fern and I'm going to feed you to Daisy.

*(**PEARL** picks up the telephone. To all the cats:)*

I'm going to call Daisy, I got Daisy on the phone, Here comes Daisy, Daisy's coming! *(She watches them all scatter. Chuckles. Replaces the phone.)* Look at them all run and hide. Daisy is the Pit-bull who lives next door, they hate her. I say her name and they all run and hide. Tough love. It's mean but it works. Of course, I'm not one of these people who likes cats and hates dogs, I'm really not. I go both ways. Most people do. You can quote me on that. But, life dealt me cats and here I am. I couldn't bring a dog into it now, they'd go crazy. You know what the difference is, between a cat and a dog? You have a dog, right? And he thinks: "My good-ness, this person feeds me and takes care of me and gives me a home. They must be a God!" A cat, on the other hand, thinks: "My goodness, this person feeds me and takes care of me and gives me a home…" I must be a God!

(She laughs, which turns into a coughing fit.)

Excuse me. Believe me, that's nothing, you should have heard me when I smoked three packs of Menthol Lights a day. I sounded like a crow with indigestion. Of course, that's when I was working in the biz and run-ning around with all the Smurfs. Oh, I would get up at 8 a.m., light a cigarette, shut off my alarm, and then I'd get my copy of *Variety* and I'd read it cover to cover, starting at the back with the obits, you always want to know who died first. Oh, I have seen my friends drink themselves to death, drug themselves to death, kill themselves…and all because they didn't know how to survive in the biz…What's the biz? Oh, dear, the only biz: Show Biz! I was a theatrical manager before I retired…*(suddenly turning her focus on a cat by her chair)* Hello Helen. Hello. Well hello. Do you want to get up? Well, all right.

(She lifts Helen, with difficulty, onto her lap.)

This is Helen, the world's fattest cat. But very docile, as you can see. Here, rub her belly, it's good luck. (**SHE** *rubs Helen's belly and talks to her in baby-talk.)* Oh, she's sit-ting on the chair like the big people do… yes… *(Helen starts to scratch at her.)* Oh, all right, now. Don't get fidg-ety. *(pushes Helen off her lap)* There. Go eat something. *(to the interviewer)* Yes, dear, I was a theatrical manager before I retired. What? Oh, dear, I'm 83 years old. Well thank-you, I moisturize. And you don't look a day over 30. Oh, you are 30. Well. There you go. Believe me dear, I didn't always have this house full of cats. I was too busy working in the Biz and running around with all the Smurfs. *(pause)* The Smurfs. *(pause)* You know, those little blue people with the white hats. No, dear,

I was the road manager for "Smurfs on Ice." It was a traveling ice-skating show featuring 12 singing skating Smurfs. Oh, the children loved it. Now, I know you want to hear about the cats dear, but let me tell you about the Smurfs. It's really kind of the same thing... First of all, there were 12 them. 12 angry Smurfs; all blue, all gay, all crazy. Now, when I say crazy I mean crazy in a good way. And the fact that they were all gay was really just a fluke. When we put the ad out in the paper for 12 figure-skating, singing men to dress up like Smurfs not one heterosexual showed up. Oh, but those Smurfs...they were a hoot and a holler. "Pearl!" they used to say, "Come out dancing. We're all going to go dancing tonight!" And they would take me to these places. With the flashing lights and this horrible music. Sounded like a pack of hyenas in a Cuisinart. *(Another cat approaches her chair.)*

Hello. Well hello. Do you want to get up? Well all right. *(lifts cat onto her lap)* This is Dom, one of my Siamese cats. Look at his pretty blue eyes. And they're crossed, see? Dom when he's hungry is a scary sight. *(She imitates Dom when he's hungry and laughs and coughs.)* Do you want to see something cute? Watch this, he loves this. Come on, Dom! *(She picks up Dom and holds his front paws in the air, so he stands on his hind legs.)* Now you get him up on his paws like this. Are you ready, Dom?

*(**PEARL** makes Dom do a little dance while she sings a song, after which she releases Dom and watches him run off.)*

He doesn't really love it. Anyway, dear, I was with "Smurfs on Ice" for three and a half years. Oh, it was a lovely job. No health benefits, the pay was lousy and you worked night and day but I loved it. And those Smurfs. Let me tell you, it was a job and a half just keeping track of them all. You know, the cats and the Smurfs really do have a lot in common, besides the fact that they were my family, then and now. For one thing they were both entirely the same: *(one hand)* Cats. *(the other hand)* Smurfs. And yet they were all completely different. For example, Jerry. Jerry was the tallest Smurf and skinny as a rail but he ate nothing but lard and ice-cream all day, had the metabolism of a humming bird. And Tony. Tony had a tan no matter where we went. We'd be touring Canada in January and Tony would waltz in with a tan. I used to say: "What'd you do, Tony? Stick your face in a toaster?"

(She laughs and has a coughing fit.)

Fur ball. Oh, but Timmy. Timmy was my favorite. Little lanky red-head with freckles, he looked like a gay Opie, you just wanted to pinch him. He played Smurfette because he was so petite. And once you put those costumes on, gender just goes out the window. You're Smurf. Oh, and Timmy loved chocolate. We used to sit in the back of the tour bus, throwing M&M's at each other's mouths. "Mine's so big I don't know how you could miss!", I used to say. Oh. But then. After awhile. People just stopped believing in the Smurfs. Sales were slow. Expenses were high. And pretty soon the whole show just went belly up. Of course, it wasn't even the same show after Timmy had left. What? Oh. Well, Timmy and Dave were walking back to the motel one night. Dave played Papa Smurf. He was quiet. And it was night, but around 10:30. Not that late. And they were walking down the street. And these two men came out of no where. And one of them had a pipe. And he hit Timmy in the face with it. And he kept hitting him. Beat him into the ground. And Dave tried to stop them and they beat him up pretty badly, too. Gave him a concussion. But Timmy. Oh, it was terrible. He was black and blue all over. And I've seen him blue. Timmy was this big, *(pinches her fingers together)* for goodness sake, I could wear him in my lapel, he wouldn't hurt a fly. And or course I thought it was my fault…somehow, I should have been there…I hadn't been doing my job properly. *(pause)* The doctor said that the first blow had burst a blood vessel in Timmy's eye so he wouldn't be able to see out of it for awhile. He would just have to rest and wait for the blood to drain out. They said he was lucky he could see at all. *(pause)* I brought Timmy a pint of chocolate-chocolate chip Haagen Dazs and he looked better. He was getting better every day. But... he couldn't do the show anymore. The doctors said even after he left the hospital, no strenuous physical activity for at least six months. So, Timmy packed up and went back home to Omaha. And after that the show just kind of sank. Which is too bad because those Smurfs were very ahead of their time. You know that Blue Man Group that's playing now? It's the Smurfs with drums, I swear to goodness. So, all my Smurfs packed up and said good-bye and went their separate ways and I came back here, to this empty house. It was empty then if you can believe it. And I got bored. So I got a cat. Marcy. She was my first cat. And then I got Dave and Tony and Rick and Celine and Shelly and Phil and oh, I just kept getting cats until something clicked and my stress level was back to normal. *(pause)* Because I don't want to be some old lady, sitting around, waiting to die. *(She smiles.)* And you know what? The Smurfs still call me on my birthday. Each one of them. No matter where they are. Because they are all good boys. *(pause)* Well, that's it for me, dear. I'm happy, I'm alive, I have all my cats. But what about you? Tell me all about yourself. I'm sure it's all quite fascinating.

(Music. Fade to black.)

END

DREAM OF
JEANNIE BY-THE-DOOR

By David Valdes Greenwood

CHARACTERS

BONNIE – A young bride.
GARY – A young groom.
WILMA – A very senior citizen.

SETTING

A casino somewhere. The present.

*(**GARY** and **BONNIE**, each maybe 20 years-old, sit side by side facing forward. Between them and us, and unseen, are slot machines. **GARY** wears a cowboy hat and tuxedo. **BONNIE** wears a wedding dress. They appear to be pulling slots and are a bit zombie-like from repetition. Each holds a plastic coin cup in a free hand, and several more cups surround their feet. There is an empty stool next to them, indicating an open slot.)*

*(**WILMA**, older than God, wearing a cheery track suit ensemble and sneakers, hurries in, clutching a coin cup. Clearly anxious to find her spot, she sees the stool and could cry or sing from relief.)*

WILMA. Oh thank God! *(Speaking in a looping speedy whirlwind, she addresses **GARY** who does not make eye contact.)* I missed the first senior shuttle and was just beside myself – what if "I Dream of Jeannie" by-the-door was gone? I could see it: a stranger. A tourist in my seat! I hate that. Oh sure, I could adjust, I'm a tough old bird, believe you me, I can sit at "Reel 'em In" next-to-the-Ladies-Room or even Monopoly by-the-change-kiosk, but it isn't the same, and I lose my touch, and I might as well stay home and watch Animal Vets on cable. *(Breath. Beat. A real look at them.)* Married long?

*(**GARY** just looks at **WILMA**, **BONNIE** doesn't even blink, and **GARY** turns his eyes forward again. As if in sync, they both pull. We hear the sound of small change falling. **BONNIE** has won, but not much.)*

GARY. How'd ya do?

BONNIE. *(Eyes forward. When **BONNIE** speaks, it's a rare and harsh burst.)* CRAP.

*(**GARY** reaches into her coin cup and takes a few coins, but makes it obvious he is only taking a portion.)*

WILMA. Oh isn't that nice! My husband would've just grabbed the lot of it, cause he always knew I wasn't so good with money – he used to take my paycheck from the shoe shop even, so I wouldn't lost track of it, such a smart thing to do – that's how we bought a house! Even so, I wouldnta minded sometimes keeping a little more. 'Course nowadays things are so different. You probably have one of those Pre-Nuptial things like on tv, right?

(**GARY** *rolls his eyes in disbelief. Both pull. No win. Briefest deflation. But not for long.*)

WILMA. *(To* **BONNIE***)* Do you wear that every day, dear? There's a lady who always plays the Roulette by-the-fountain, and her lucky outfit is a Chinese kimono – or is that Japanese? I don't know, but a kimono alright – all dragons on silk, and she's as Black as they come, which doesn't seem very Chinese to me, but it makes her lucky, you bet, or she wouldn't do it. I bet you have a good story for that dress, huh? *(nothing)* Awfully pretty, though I would think it won't keep if you wear it to Stop 'n Shop and bingo and, you know, all the time. Or do you just change into it when you get here? It looks hard to clean –

BONNIE. *(not looking at* **WILMA***, but with a terrifying voice)* IT'S GODDAMN FUCKING FINE.

GARY. *(A look at* **WILMA***)* Jeezus, Lady.

WILMA. Oh dear, too nosy, oh – I just, well, I get so curious, so many people do interesting things for luck, and –

GARY. *(hushing her)* She doesn't wear it for luck. Alright? It's her wedding dress.

WILMA. Oh my, is today your –

GARY. Unh uh.

WILMA. No?

GARY. Not today.

WILMA. But –

GARY. Sunday.

WILMA. Today *is* Sunday.

(GARY glares at her then turns back to his slot. He seems to indicate something behind him; WILMA is baffled and then gets it – they have been there a week.)

WILMA. Oh, well then. Happy anniversary-ish! *(Beat. Pulls. Nothing. A look at them. Pulls. Nothing. Can't resist.)* So where are you honeymooning? **(GARY** *glares.* **BONNIE** *lifts her skirt – their luggage is hidden underneath.)* Oh, how nice! I love it here. Alfred and I went to Atlantic City, back when it was still really something – Miss America used to be there, you know! Boy that place had it all: craps, bingo, beaches, lobster, roulette, dancing, slots – course that was so far and now you got places close to home, like they should be. Something for everyone. You ask me, if every town had one of these, there'd be no crime! *(beat)* You kids from around here?

GARY. Event security. *(nods at Bonnie)* Steakhouse.

WILMA. Oh, I meant – well, isn't that nice anyway. *(tries a new tack)* So, do your folks *live* around here?

(They don't answer. **GARY** *looks nervous. He pulls.)*

WILMA. Do your –

BONNIE. MY MOTHER FUCKING DROWNED.

WILMA. Oh dear, that's just awful!

GARY. *(whispers)* Out back. The river behind the casino.

WILMA. Oh no, that's a beautiful river – unless of course your mother drowns in it. *(sotto voce to* **GARY***)* Truth to tell, I can't imagine why the poor thing would've been swimming there at all, I mean, since the factory dumping it's not even fit for catfish, let alone –

GARY. She wasn't *swimming.* Jeez, lady.

WILMA. Ah. *(stuck)* Well, then.

(Everybody pulls. Nobody wins. Silence on all. Distant bells and casino noise.)

*(***BONNIE*** pulls again and wins a few more coins – holds her cup up without evident joy.)*

WILMA. Alfred went that way, you know. Not drowning, but you know, got up one morning and said, "Enough." Not out loud, I suppose, and not to me, but all the same. Used to be a nuclear engineer at the shipyard – bet you had people there, too, right? Oh he loved that job. We went to every boat christening for just about forever.

His job paid so good those days that when we had our little girl, I could afford to just quit, and stay home with her, right up till she was old enough to run off to an ashram and forget us. That was hard – home alone while he had somewhere to go every day, and he knew I was at loose ends, and finally let me have a little money of my own, said I'd earned it. Got an allowance every week, which I mostly used for scratch tickets – this was before we had our own casinos, of course – and I played Bingo, I guess you could say those were my hobbies. Alfred never needed hobbies, cause he had the shipyard – played on the ball team there, organized the employee picnic. He had his thing and I had mine.

Oh, he took it awful hard when the yard closed. Nothing worse around the house than a man, let me tell you. So you can imagine I thought it was a real blessing when this place opened. Not just for me, though I can't say I wasn't excited about real slots right here in my own town. But it meant a job for him and all the fellas from the yard, not to mention the gals from the shoe shop which closed down, oh ages before that, and the folks from the big grocery that went under. Easy job, easy to get to work – I thought: well, he's *saved*. But he never took to it.

'Course, it was about a twelfth of his old pay and wouldn't you know my expenses went up. He was just crabby all the time then. I used to say, "Alfred, it's a gift for a man your age. Just relax and enjoy it – play a game, *sit* with me!" (*She looks at* **GARY** *and* **BONNIE** *wistfully.*) I don't know why he couldn't just be happy. I am. (*Beat. Nothing*) So.

*(Everybody pulls. **BONNIE** wins bigger. Lots of change we can't see seems to be spilling toward **BONNIE** who seems to fill her cup and then a bit of **GARY***'s.)*

WILMA. Oh MY. Well isn't that nice?

GARY. Good job, honey –

*(**GARY** rises, ready to celebrate.)*

WILMA. There must be fifty dollars!

*(**GARY** freezes.)*

GARY. What? No – it's more, obviously. Look –

WILMA. Oh, I'm an expert – I'd say you have about two hundred quarters there. I've seen a lot of $50 winners in my day. Only happened to me once so far, I still remember it: first day I ever wore these sneakers so now I wear them every time and –

BONNIE. GODDAMMIT.

WILMA. What? *(looks at her feet)* They smell. Do they smell?

GARY. It just – it just looks like a LOT of money.

WILMA. Oh no, the serious money makes a lot more noise, and the lights don't stop, and you can hardly keep up with the quarters which are really just for show anyway cause they'll send a Manager over to explain how much more you get that would never fit into a cup. *(This is so dreamy, **WILMA** can hardly describe it.)* And everybody looks at you and they're all so cause it's your time, it's your time, and you feel a kind of a hush even though the bells just keep ringing and ringing – oh, it's heaven! *(**GARY** and **BONNIE** look destroyed. **WILMA** sees this, realizes her mistake.)* But this is good too! You can go get yourself a nice meal at one of the celebrity restaurants. Take a break, you've earned it!

*(**BONNIE** grabs her cup close and shrieks.)*

BONNIE. NOOOOOOOO!

*(**WILMA** is a bit terrified. She actually considers giving up her seat.)*

GARY. Aw jeez. *(beat)* She felt lucky. Ok? Woke up on our wedding day *lucky.* Her mother came to her in a dream. Said, "Bonnie, you can make it back. All $5,000 in one pull." 5,000 – that's why she drowned: a month's salary and the rest of a credit card. Not so much unless you live in this shithole town and it's everything you got. Bonnie, she got her job here just to make the casino give something back. Sweet-talks herself some killer tips from guys who blow 5,000 in one pop.

Saved every goddamn tip for two years for our honeymoon. To Disneyland, supposed to be. Booked the hotel that's done up in Pirate stuff. Gonna go on rides. Go to Universal. The whole deal. Be as far away as we've ever been. But her mother – soaked to the bone, right, and floating on the ceiling – said "Bonnie honey, today's your lucky day. Everything gets better. Everything will be just like you imagine. You're gonna win big, lucky girl." Scary, huh? But cool. *(He means that.)*

She tells me, I'm like, Why not? Sure, people lose all the time, everyone we know, right? But people do win. They must. Or why do it at all? And if her Mom comes from the dead, says it's her day – *(Shrugs.)* I mean, we had a few hours before they expected us at the church.

WILMA. You came *before?*

GARY. She won on the first pull. It was magic, right? You know that feeling? My seat was cold – nothing going on here. But she had it. You could tell. And you don't blow that. I mean, voice from the dead, right? So we kinda…stayed.

WILMA. With everyone waiting for you?

GARY. When we win, they'll understand.

WILMA. Well, sure, everybody wants to win, but all the same, it doesn't seem very *social.*

(Enough. **BONNIE** *begins to come unglued.)*

BONNIE. DON'T FUCKING CRITICIZE ME!

WILMA. I just –

BONNIE. YOU'RE BREAKING THE SPELL!

GARY. No, honey, it's ok –

BONNIE. I'M CLOSE! I'M CLOSE!

GARY. Baby –

(The fun stops here.)

BONNIE. *(To* **WILMA***)* THIS IS THE BEST THING I'VE EVER FUCKING DONE AND I'VE WAITED MY WHOLE LIFE FOR THIS AND I WILL KILL YOU IF YOU RUIN THIS FOR ME, YOU MISERABLE FUCKING CUNT. THIS IS A CASINO, GODDAMMIT, SO SHUT YOUR HOLE AND GAMBLE.

(Silence. **WILMA** *takes this in, with the pinched grace of the old.)*

WILMA. *(To* **GARY***)* Well, you got yourself a live one there.

GARY. Isn't she something?

(They all pull. **BONNIE** *looks unhinged, but dry eyed. Fierce.)*

(Pull.)

(Pull.)

(Pull.)

(And then bells. Lights racing.)

*(***BONNIE** *has won and the noise doesn't stop.)*

*(***GARY** *and* **WILMA** *rise.* **WILMA** *hands over her cup, as* **GARY** *tries to catch the endless unseen coins. He sees someone coming across the casino and cannot believe it has happened.)*

GARY. The guy – they're sending *the guy*! You did it, Baby!

(It's everything they want and it doesn't do the trick at all. **BONNIE** *begins to weep; the enormity of her loss cannot be caught in a change cup.)*

*(***WILMA** *cannot see this, and goes to her, rubbing her, like a magic lamp, touching herself with the hand that touched* **BONNIE.** *)*

(**BONNIE** *howls.* **GARY** *gets it, drops the cup. Freezes, as if to say: Shit.*)

(**BONNIE** *is bereft. But* **WILMA**, *missing the whole thing, is positively inspired.*)

WILMA. I know, I know. *(rushes back to her slot machine for a good pull)* It feels *good*, doesn't it?

(Black.)

INTIMATE APPAREL

By William Cunningham

CHARACTERS

Marjorie
Ken
Anita

SETTING

The Lingerie Store.

(SCENE: The Lingerie Store.)

(MARJORIE and ANITA enter.)

MARJORIE. I thought we weren't packaging ourselves in pink anymore?

ANITA. Don't be difficult, Marjorie. You can't out-shop her. You can't overpower her. So that leaves us with...

MARJORIE. Underwear?

ANITA. Undergarments. A Ken wants his Barbie packaged in pink.

MARJORIE. He is not a *Ken*! He is a *Stephen*!

ANITA. Stephen is playing house, Marjorie, with another woman.

MARJORIE. So *you* say!

ANITA. What did Stephen say? Till death do us part? Fidelity? Faithfulness? Words. We've all heard them. I'm through with words. Time for action.

MARJORIE. Have you seen the price of...

ANITA. Revenge, Marjorie. It's going to require that we use all of our equipment, everything in our arsenal.

MARJORIE. I'm not sure my arsenal will fit into any of these...I was Phi Bata Kappa, Marjorie. Just like you. We helped develop each other's resume, cataloguing our saleable qualities, and we didn't then – and we don't now – have to resort to...padding.

ANITA. Substance doesn't always win out, Marjorie. Wife and mother. Look how that turned out.

MARJORIE. So I should give over to...

ANITA. Material. Because to them – to men – it is all about material. Silk and lace. Pick up lines. Possessions. Do you think they care about GPAs or academic transcripts? Stockings and gloves and garter belts, those grab their attention.

MARJORIE. Are you saying that she is…

ANITA. A desirable object.

MARJORIE. And I should be…?

ANITA. An object with the ability to attract.

MARJORIE. Or repel.

ANITA. Opposing forces, Marjorie. In order to repel her, you need to become an impenetrable object.

MARJORIE. *(turning to the merchandise)* Intimate apparel.

ANITA. You can put it on and you can take it off.

MARJORIE. What?

ANITA. Intimacy.

> *(A **KEN** enters. He acts nonchalant but clearly he is uncomfortable, almost intimidated by the wardrobe of fantasy.)*

MARJORIE. I can't, Anita.

ANITA. You can.

MARJORIE. I'm not this type of action figure. It's…

ANITA. Technology, Marjorie. Imported Lycra spandex. Micro-fibers. This is modern design. Scientific advancement. We can break the laws of physics with suspension cups.

MARJORIE. Miracle bras.

KEN. *(to an unseen presence)* I'm just looking.

ANITA. Amen for Miracle bras.

KEN. Window shopping.

ANITA. If you can't be a hard target, Marjorie, you have no choice but to be a soft one.

KEN. I thought…maybe…I would like…That is *my wife* would like…Pajamas? They would be…? Over…? Thank you.

ANITA. Try it.

MARJORIE. It?

ANITA. On him.

KEN. I'm just looking.

MARJORIE. *(quietly to* **ANITA***)* I don't know him.

ANITA. How well do you know anyone? Be engaging.

MARJORIE. Revenge is...

ANITA. ...sweet, Marjorie. Just be sweet.

(pushing her in that direction)

MARJORIE. You're looking for...?

KEN. Pajamas.

MARJORIE. Pajamas for...?

KEN. My wife.

MARJORIE. That's...

ANITA. *(quietly to* **MARJORIE***)* Sweet.

KEN. I was looking for something...

MARJORIE. Spicy?

KEN. Yes.

MARJORIE. Tangy?

KEN. Tangy?

ANITA. *(quietly to* **MARJORIE***)* Stop cooking.

MARJORIE. Lacy.

KEN. Yes.

MARJORIE. What size?

KEN. Size?

MARJORIE. Is your wife.

KEN. She's about...

MARJORIE. My...?

KEN. Petite, but...

MARJORIE. More...

KEN. Full...

MARJORIE. ...er?

KEN. Perhaps I should...It's not that these aren't...

ANITA. *(quietly to* **ANITA***)* Tempting.

KEN. It's just that my wife, you see, is more conservative... more subdued.

ANITA. *(quietly to* **MARJORIE***)* The inhibited type.

KEN. Believe me, she wouldn't be...

MARJORIE. Comfortable.

KEN. In lounge wear...Yes...She's just as happy with...

MARJORIE. Discount?

KEN. ...pajamas...No...I mean, it's not as if I'm...

MARJORIE. Devaluing her?

ANITA. *(quietly to* **MARJORIE***)* Get off economics.

KEN. I'm not!...I'm just...

MARJORIE. Thinking.

KEN. Of her! Of my wife!...I wouldn't want my wife – her – thinking that I'm thinking...Because I'm not...

MARJORIE. Thinking.

KEN. I'm looking!...for...you know...something...

MARJORIE. Else.

KEN. What am I thinking?

ANITA. *(quietly to* **MARJORIE***)* Personalize it.

MARJORIE. What's your name?

KEN. Scott.

MARJORIE. Scott.

ANITA. *(quietly to* **MARJORIE***)* Is a very...

MARJORIE. Strong name.

KEN. No, it isn't.

MARJORIE. Strong?

KEN. My name. My name isn't Scott. I don't know why I told you that my name was Scott. Because it isn't. Why would I...?

MARJORIE. Take on a new identity?

KEN. Why would I do that?

MARJORIE. You want...

KEN. *Pajamas!* I swear to you, I came in here looking... around...

ANITA. *(quietly to* **MARJORIE***)* Offer him a selection.

KEN. ...browsing...for a simple pair of warm pajamas!... Is it hot in here?...You see, the truth is there is a need for warmth in our house. You see, it isn't snug...not as snug as it should be...which isn't to say that it isn't comfortable. Because it's comfortable. It's very comfortable. But drafty. There's a draft. Do you have anything in flannel?

ANITA. *(quietly to* **MARJORIE***)* We don't sell flannel.

MARJORIE. You didn't come in here for flannel.

KEN. I didn't?

MARJORIE. You came in for something soft...

KEN. I did?

MARJORIE. Something sheer, something cotton, something meshy.

KEN. I don't want to get tangled in anything meshy.

MARJORIE. Embroidered.

KEN. That sounds so...

MARJORIE. Seductive...Isn't that why you came in here? Aren't you looking for something...

KEN. Erogenous...*erroneous*!...What?

MARJORIE. I didn't say anything.

KEN. Jesus, it's hot in here...Listen...O.K...I'm looking... around...the mall. Drifting, from store to store. Checking out a Sharper Image here, a Hallmark there. The Limited is so...and Structure isn't for me. I find myself in Borders. I've spent way too much time in Borders. So, I wander in here. Where's the harm if an All-American Joe like me wanders in here, looking...

MARJORIE. Checking out...

KEN. It's legal!...to look.

ANITA. *(quietly to* **MARJORIE***)* But he better not touch.

KEN. We tell ourselves that we won't become consigned, departmentalized. And one day we find ourselves buying off the rack. We find ourselves suddenly out of fashion, saving our money so that we can raise Gap Kids. I've earned...I've paid...the bills...the debts... I have the right to expect...Promises were made! Dreams are supposed to come due!...My wife, she is...

MARJORIE. Real.

KEN. A flesh and blood bargain shopper. Was I wrong to expect…?

ANITA. One that requires no visual means of support.

KEN. You're selling fantasy here. I want…I'll purchase… I'll take on credit…what I've seen wiggling across my screen, laid out in my magazines, parading by with their wings…angels. I have seen heavenly angels in this store, angels for sale.

(sinking to his knees)

Please…What does it cost? What's the price of dressing up the truth? To believe that I could be the object of someone's desire? What does that cost? Because I'll pay, any price…God help me…*I want thongs!*

(**MARJORIE** *puts her hand on* **KEN** *'s face.*)

MARJORIE. I'll call you…Stephen.

KEN. And you? You are…?

MARJORIE. I haven't decided yet.

(Blackout.)

CPSIA information can be obtained
at www.ICGtesting.com
Printed in the USA
LVHW08s2103310818
588764LV00009B/39/P